David Livingstone

Tim & Linda Shubert
22428 SR 119
Goshen, IN 46526-7479

THIS

BOOK

BELONGS TO:

David Livingstone

by
Fern Neal Stocker

A Guessing Book

MOODY PRESS
CHICAGO

© 1986 by
THE MOODY BIBLE INSTITUTE
OF CHICAGO

All rights reserved. No part of this book may be reproduced in any form without permission in writing from the publisher, except in the case of brief quotations embodied in critical articles or reviews.

All Scripture quotations are from the King James Version.

Illustrations are by Virginia Hughins.

Library of Congress Cataloging in Publication Data

Stocker, Fern Neal, 1917-
    David Livingstone.

    (A Guessing Book)
    Summary: Examines the life of the Scotsman who
explored large portions of Africa and brought thousands
of people to Christ. At intervals in the text the
reader finds a question followed by several possible
answers, one or more of which may be correct.
    1. Livingstone, David, 1813-1873—Juvenile literature.
2. Explorers—Africa, Southern—Biography—Juvenile
literature. 3. Explorers—Scotland—Biography—
Juvenile literature. 4. Missionaries, Medical—Africa,
Southern—Biography—Juvenile literature.
5. Missionaries, Medical—Scotland—Biography—Juvenile
literature. [1. Livingstone, David, 1813-1873.
2.   3. Missionaries. 4. Literary recreations]
I. Title. II. Series:
Stocker, Fern
Neal, 1917-   . Guessing book.
DT731.L8S78 1986   916.7′04′0924 [B]   86-21732
ISBN 0-8024-4758-9 (pbk.)

3 4 5 6 7 Printing/LC/Year 91 90 89 88 87

Printed in the United States of America

To Tami and Shellie Stocker

Contents

To You, the Reader:

A Guessing Book is the story of a famous person. As you read along in this Guessing Book, you'll come to questions you can answer by yourself.

One, two, or three guesses are given, and you can choose one, two, or three answers. Sometimes all are correct, sometimes none. (You'll find the answer as you keep reading.) Pretty soon you'll know the person in the story so well you can get the answer right every time.

It may be fun to keep track of how many guesses you get right. But if you miss one, don't worry—this isn't a test.

Read this Guessing Book and learn about David Livingstone, a man who wanted to glorify God, not himself.

1

Shuttle Row

David and John scuttled down two flights of spiral stairways with their empty wooden buckets.

They were going to

GUESS

1. the store.
2. the well.
3. the cotton mill.

It was 1825, and they were on their way to work in the cotton mill. The sky was lightening. In winter it was still dark when they went to work.

They carried the wooden buckets

GUESS

1. to the mill.
2. to the well.
3. to the bottom step.

David and John left their buckets on the bottom step. The next family member to go upstairs would fill a bucket at the well and carry it up to the third floor apartment. Mother always needed water for something.

A mud puddle stood in the path of John and David. John, the older brother, walked around it. David

GUESS	1. also walked around it.
	2. stamped his feet in the water.
	3. didn't see it.

David stamped his feet in the water.

"You are twelve years old—too old for such foolishness," John reproved.

"I'll soon dry in the hot mill," David answered. "Race you!"

The boys ran down the hill and across Shuttle Row to the Blantrye Works. As usual, John won the race, but David didn't care. He wanted an excuse to run. He viewed the river and its green banks. *Some day I'll climb up there and see what is on the other side,* he promised himself.

Both boys worked in the spinning room of the cotton mill. Each was assigned a section of machines, and they were soon at work.

David's job was as

GUESS	1. a spinner.
	2. a piecer.
	3. a cutter.

Children from ten to seventeen years of age worked as piecers in the mills in Scotland in 1825.

A piecer

GUESS	1. tied knots in thread.
	2. mended broken cotton ropes.
	3. stacked pieces of thread in piles.

David found broken places in the cotton batten ropes and lightly pressed the moist ends back together. He gave the ends a slight roll between his thumb and finger so the cotton would stick together.

The work was

GUESS	1. heavy.
	2. difficult.
	3. easy.

It was easy work. The trouble was with the walking. David had to walk every minute to look for breaks in the yarn. He walked

GUESS	1. two miles a day.
	2. ten miles a day.
	3. twenty miles a day.

Piecers walked at least twenty miles a day. David was used to it; he had already been working two years. Round and round the machines he trudged. The machines he worked with were called

GUESS	1. spinning jennys.
	2. spinning wheels.
	3. spinning jims.

The new machines were called spinning jennys, and they could spin eight strands of yarn at the same time. (The old spinning wheels could only make one strand of yarn from a rope of cotton batten.) That meant that David had to watch eight strands on every machine. If one broke, he pieced it together again. He was supposed to piece it at once, so every one of the eight strands would be the same length.

David had twenty machines to watch, so he had

GUESS	1. 40 strands to keep together.
	2. 100 strands to keep together.
	3. 160 ropes to mend.

He had 160 ropes of cotton batten to piece back together when they broke. Sometimes many broke at the same time, and David's legs flew as he raced from one to the other. The words of the supervisor haunted him. "Be ye the cause of short bobbins that make bad cord, ye be fired, David. Mind you look sharp and walk steady."

David did not want to be fired, because

GUESS

1. Mother needed the money from his wages.
2. in order to live in their apartment, someone had to work in the mill.
3. David would be ashamed to fail.

All of those things were true. Since Father was a tea merchant, it was up to the children to work in the mill so that the family would have a home.

As Mr. Livingstone delivered his tea to the homes of his customers, he also

GUESS

1. carried the gossip.
2. gave away gospel tracts.
3. made enemies.

Mr. Livingstone was a Christian and gave away gospel tracts. He felt he was doing God's will.

David

GUESS

1. loved his father.
2. thought his father was too strict.
3. hated his father.

All the Livingstone children loved their father but feared his anger. They tried to follow his strict rules.

At noon David was free for an hour. He ate his lunch of oatcakes and

GUESS	1. played hide-and-seek.
	2. daydreamed.
	3. threw water on John.

Sometimes he played with the boys; sometimes he daydreamed in the sunshine; and sometimes he explored the mill. After a few years, David knew what happened to the cotton from the time it arrived from America till it was shipped out as rope, cord, or fishnets.

" 'Tis enough to put your eye out to see all the steps it takes to make a fishnet out of cotton," David marveled.

The whistle blew at five, and David and John stopped their work and ran

GUESS	1. toward home.
	2. to town.
	3. to a restaurant.

The brothers ran toward home. It wasn't far across Shuttle Row, but they knew

GUESS	1. a running start helped climb the hills.
	2. it would soon be dark.
	3. Mother would have a hot supper ready.

They were hungry, and Mother always had a hot meal ready (the Scots called it "feed").

While running, David looked up at the apartment house. It was

GUESS	1. three stories high.
	2. ten stories high.
	3. all on one floor.

It was three stories high with twenty-four apartments. One could see the spiral staircases on the outside of the building. There were

15

GUESS
1. two staircases.
2. three staircases.
3. four staircases.

Four staircases could be seen. David was glad their apartment was on the top floor, because

GUESS
1. it smelled better.
2. there was a beautiful view.
3. they could carry the water bucket farther.

Although David and John grew tired of carrying the wooden buckets to the top floor, David loved the view. From there he could see

GUESS
1. the mill.
2. the River Clyde.
3. the sloping green hillside.

The mill couldn't spoil the sight of the crashing River Clyde or the many shades of green on the hillside.

The boys filled the buckets, climbed the stairs, and burst into the warm room filled with the good smell of roasting lamb.

"Wash your hands, laddies," Mother greeted.

"And hurry, we been waiting and waiting," wailed Janet, their younger sister.

"Don't complain. The boys came as soon as the whistle blew." Father defended them.

David played peekaboo with Agnes while he waited for John. She giggled loudly.

At the table, all seven joined hands, and Father asked Janet to say the blessing. She prayed

GUESS
1. a memorized prayer.
2. a long thanksgiving.

3. a short prayer.

Janet prayed in a few words. She was eight and saw no need for a long prayer.

At the table everyone

| GUESS |

1. talked a lot.
2. was silent.
3. laughed and giggled.

At the Livingstone table, there was silence. Mother put the food on the plates, and Father passed the coarse bread and cheese. Only Agnes broke the silence, beating the table with her spoon and giggling when David looked at her.

Charlie was hiding food to give to a favorite neighborhood dog. He was hoping Father would not ask him any questions. He went to school all day with Janet, and sometimes Father wanted to know what he was learning.

When the meal was over, dessert was served. It was

| GUESS |

1. ice cream.
2. pie.
3. oat cookies.

They felt fortunate. Not all families could afford oat cookies for dessert.

After the Bible reading and prayer, Father said, "I am bursting to tell you the news!"

"What news?" David could not resist asking.

"I'll be telling ye, if ye let me!" Everyone looked at him, waiting.

"Grandfather wants you boys to scour the hills and valleys in search of wild flowers, ferns, and mosses. The society pays for the samples when ye send them in."

This time he didn't have to ask for silence. Everyone was stunned.

17

Mother spoke, " 'Tis time, boys. Your supper hour is almost gone, and you must not be late for your last two hours at the mill."

"Come on, David. Hurry!"

David jumped over a bench as he streaked out the door.

David was

GUESS	1. thrilled to be a collector.
	2. surprised Grandfather would trust him.
	3. excited about the spending money.

David loved collecting and classifying plants and rocks. He thought the money would go for family expenses.

2

Expedition

David got a chance to look for samples sooner then he expected.

He didn't go to the mill

GUESS

1. because he said he was sick.
2. because the steam engines broke down.
3. because he was tired of working every day.

The only vacation David ever got was when the newly invented steam engines broke down. Charles begged to look for samples, too, and Mother agreed he could go.

Charles trotted down hill cheerfully until they reached the swinging foot bridge over the River Clyde. The bridge was only wide enough for one or two people.

Charles objected

GUESS

1. to the holes between the ropes.
2. to the swinging motion.
3. to the river below.

"Every time I step, the bridge moves!" Charles cried, pulling his foot back.

"Come on, you have to step on the ropes to get across," David coaxed. "Don't look down—that's scary."

When Charles refused, David said,

1. "Go back home, then."

2. "We'll never get to the other side standing here."

3. "Come step with me. I'll keep you from falling."

Charles ventured a few steps with David. Since he didn't fall, he clung tightly to David and finally reached the other side.

David took an oat cake out of the lunch bucket for Charles. "Good lad!" he said. "If you never try anything new, you never learn."

Since working with Grandfather, David had learned about dozens of rare lichens, pink myrtle, purple heather, and privet berries. "Some day I'll be able to press flowers between glass as neatly as Grandfather," he boasted.

The cool breeze touched their sun-warmed cheeks as they climbed. When they topped the hill, they met gray clouds.

They saw

1. an old castle.

2. an airplane.

3. two golden dragons.

"There it is—Bothwell castle—deserted and decaying. We'll collect samples on the way down to the valleys and stop at the castle to eat lunch."

Charles brought dozens of flowers, twigs, and leaves to David. "Oh, laddie," David declared, "Grandfather only wants the special samples, not every old weed."

"Is this an old weed?" asked Charles, somewhat daunted.

It proved to be

1. a dandelion.

GUESS 2. a rare wild mignonette.
3. a heather.

"There it is. See the picture in the book?" David pointed. "Charlie, laddie, you've found a rare wild mignonette."

"Now can we go to the castle?"

"Yes. Grandfather will consider the trip worthwhile for this one great sample." David packed it carefully and ran with Charles the rest of the way.

They ate their lamb and oat cakes sitting near the castle wall.

"See the names carved on the castle wall, David."

The name carved highest was

GUESS 1. Skinny Flinn.
2. Queen Mary.
3. Abraham Lincoln.

"Skinny Flinn! Why he's an old man working in the mill. He must have carved his name when he was just a lad. The highest of all!" David walked over to the wall. He could see where the boys had placed their toes to climb.

David resolved to

GUESS 1. carve his name higher than Skinny Flinn.
2. dig a cave.
3. knock down the fountain.

I can carve my name with the knife from the lunch basket, he thought.

Climbing carefully, he made his way up the old wall. "If I can get to the ledge, I'll have something to stand on. Then I can make my name the largest as well as the highest." While the sun shone from the east, the dry moss helped to hold his feet.

Once on the ledge, he started with a large D-A-V. His legs began to cramp. "Oh, why did I start so big, with such a long name? Where's Charlie? Must be doing something bad; he's so quiet."

Chip, chip, chip. David hacked away. "If these bricks were new, they wouldn't break so easy." David was deep in thought when

GUESS
1. it began to rain.
2. he fell to the ground.
3. Charlie fell into an old well.

"David, David, come down! 'Tis going to rain." Charles rushed toward the wall. "Come inside, or you'll get wet!"
David

GUESS
1. hurried down.
2. kept on working in the rain.
3. quit carving and went home.

"I can't stop; I'm not finished. Go inside, Charlie. You know these showers don't last long on a day like this."

The carving continued. I-D L-I-V. "If only I could step back, I wouldn't be so cramped."

David glanced down and almost lost his breath. "Didn't know I was so high!" he gasped and hurried his carving. I-N-G-S. By now the wall was in the shadow, and David was

GUESS
1. cold.
2. sick.
3. shaking.

David was shaking with cold when Charlie announced,

GUESS
1. "I'm coming up, David."
2. "I'm going home by myself."
3. "Wake me when you're done."

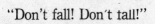

"Don't fall! Don't tall!"

"No, no, Charles, don't come up here. You'll get kilt!"

"Well, you're not kilt," Charles pointed out as he backed down.

T-O-N-E. Chip, chip, chip, and David was finished. His legs were throbbing with pain when he began his descent.

The rain had made the moss slippery, and David's foot slipped. Frantically he clung with his hands as the knife fell. Fortunately one foot was still on the ledge. " 'Twas foolish to come up so high," he muttered.

With a pounding heart, David tested each foot to see if he could balance on the slippery moss before he let go with his hands. Suddenly both feet skidded out from under him. His hands clung to the bricks, and David

1. was filled with terror and panic.
2. remembered a Bible verse and prayed.
3. was falling.

Fear gripped David while his feet searched for a new foothold. "What time I am afraid, I will trust in thee," flashed into his mind, and peace soothed him.

Carefully his feet attained a foothold as the strength left his arms. For some time he clung to the wall. "Thank You, God!" he whispered. "Help me get down, please." His fears quieted, and he made one step at a time, carefully testing each clump of moss before trusting it with his weight.

Reaching the bottom, he said,

GUESS

1. "Thank You, God."
2. "I won't be doing that again."
3. "Oh, that was fun."

David promised God not to do that again. He knew God had taken care of him.

3

What's in a Name?

Attending church was a habit for the Livingstone family. Since Father liked the church in Hamilton rather than Blantrye, they walked

GUESS

1. a mile.
2. two miles.
3. three miles.

David didn't mind the three-mile walk. He loved to see the trees, flowers, and birds. Along the way, he

GUESS

1. raced with his brothers.
2. carried Agnes when she was tired.
3. collected samples.

Sometimes he carried Agnes at the end of the day or raced with his brothers, but he loved collecting samples for Grandfather best.

Usually David managed to stay out of trouble during the services. During the long sermon, he often

| GUESS |

1. studied his spelling words.
2. learned definitions.
3. memorized Latin verbs.

He would steal a glance now and then at a scrap of paper in his hand and study.

Another thing he liked about the Hamilton church was Jeremy.

| GUESS |

1. Jeremy was his best friend.
2. Jeremy was the preacher.
3. Jeremy was a monkey.

David had some friends among the boys who worked in the mill, but none he liked as much as Jeremy. Though Jeremy was a year older, he seemed about the same age. Since both their fathers were elders in the church, the young lads played together between the morning and evening services.

"I don't see how you make your grade every year working ten hours a day," Jeremy marveled. "I go to school all day and don't learn any more."

"You don't study as much as I do." David laughed. "I have a book sitting on one of the machines. Every time I go by that machine, I read a line or two. By the time I come back, I know it by heart."

"If you work ten hours a day, when do you go to school?" Jeremy demanded.

David attended school

| GUESS |

1. between four and six A.M.
2. between eight and ten P.M.
3. between ten and twelve P.M.

The school for mill children was held from eight to ten P.M. The law said

1. all mill children must attend school.

26

GUESS

2. the mill must pay a teacher for two hours a day.

3. those who did not like school could stay home.

David was glad the law forced the mill to pay a teacher. He was among the few children who attended.

Many people wanted David to get an education, including

GUESS

1. his father and mother.

2. his grandparents.

3. his church teacher.

4. the pastor.

All those were interested in David's education. They were all interested in his behavior, also. Usually that wasn't a problem, but once he and Jeremy were sitting together in church after receiving little cards in their class. The card showed a picture of a camel on his knees with his back legs straight, as though he were about to stand up.

Jeremy drew

GUESS

1. a mustache on the camel.

2. a toboggan on the camel's back.

3. horns on the camel.

Jeremy drew a toboggan; then he made a swishing noise with his finger, as though the toboggan were flying down the camel's back over the humps, along his neck, and landing on the ground.

For some reason, both Jeremy and David

GUESS

1. got sick.

2. laughed.

3. looked angelic.

Their laughter filled the church, and everyone turned to look.

Pastor Moir stopped preaching and waited. The boys couldn't stop laughing.

When they didn't stop, the preacher said, "Stand on either side of the pulpit."

David and Jeremy stood on either side of the pulpit facing the dour Scotsmen, their families, and friends. Suddenly David felt

GUESS	1. funny.
	2. clever.
	3. frightened.

Dismay and fear filled David. He was so ashamed he wished a trapdoor would open and he could fall through the earth to China.

When the preacher finally had pity on them and let them sit down, David said,

GUESS	1. "I hate you!"
	2. "I'll never face an audience again."
	3. "What was so funny?"

David vowed never, never to look into the faces of a crowd again.

As the years passed, David found the services more interesting. He did not need a songbook to sing "All People That on Earth Do Dwell." It was an old favorite metrical version of a psalm.

David's sixteenth birthday fell on a church day. It was a special day. They sang the Twenty-Third Psalm, "The Lord is my shepherd; I shall not want."

David sang, "I will fear no evil," knowing he trusted God when he was on the castle wall.

When Pastor Moir began preaching, he asked, "Why do people write their names on trees, fences, or walls?"

David pictured in his mind the castle wall.

The preacher said, "We all want to glorify ourselves. We want a name that is above every name. We want our name to be higher than all. Why? Why? Why? Because we want to glorify ourselves."

David's face became

GUESS	1. shameful.
	2. red.
	3. white.

David's face turned red, and shame filled his heart.

The pastor continued, "The reason for living is to glorify God, not ourselves. The name of Jesus is high and lifted up. At the name of Jesus every knee shall bow."

David resolved to

GUESS	1. glorify himself.
	2. glorify God.
	3. forget the sermon.

A deep resolve filled David's heart. "I'll live for Jesus. I'll glorify God, not myself. Indeed, I will."

It wasn't easy during the next week. The singing was quiet, the preaching past, and Christian friends far away. His friend Neil came to David in the mill and said, "Come, go curling* with us after work."

"But I have to go to school; I can't play," David explained.

"Why?" demanded Neil. "You want to be better'n us. You're old enough to quit school now. Nobody goes after they's sixteen."

"I do," David answered.

GUESS	1. "I'm resolved to glorify God."
	2. "I don't want to be a dummy."
	3. "I have a reason."

He muttered, "I have a reason," but somehow he couldn't say anything about God. Secretly he rejoiced when the lunch bell sounded, and he went back to work. "Someday, I'm going to have to stand up to those mill lads. I better go see Grandfather before then."

*Scottish game.

When David visited Grandfather, he was full of questions. He asked,

1. "How can I glorify God?"
2. "How can a Christian own slaves and glorify God?"
3. "How do you glorify God when you don't say it?"

David wanted to know how Grandfather managed to let everyone know he glorified God when he seldom said it.

Grandfather laughed. "People know because of

1. what you say."
2. what you do."
3. what you don't do."

Grandfather explained, "People watch what you do and pay little heed to what you say. Every morning I ask God to let people see Jesus in me."

"That's it," David explained. "The lads are always asking me to curl with them. I love the game, but school is important. When I say no they think I have my nose out of joint."

Grandfather answered,

GUESS

1. "There's nothing wrong with the game."
2. "You don't have time for play."
3. "If you are going to be a doctor, you have to study."

Grandfather reminded David of their secret plan for David to be a doctor.

"But the boys don't understand."

"They may not understand," Grandfather responded, "but if you stand firm, they'll leave you alone."

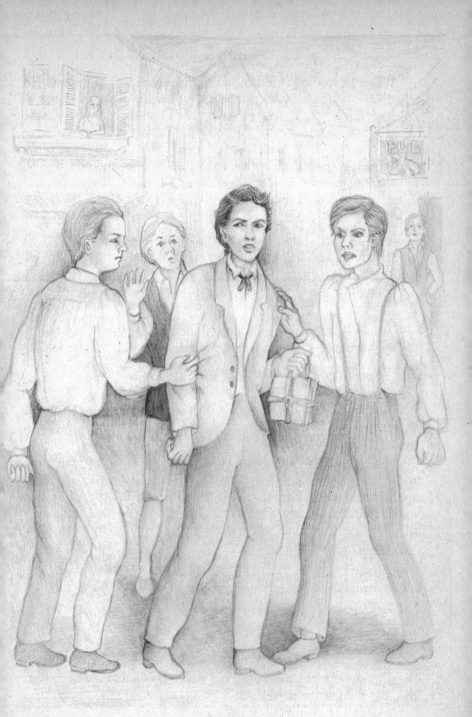

"You study too much!"

"Then I lose my friends," David objected.

"God will give you other friends—you'll see. Remember the old saying, 'Eagles fly alone, but sheep herd together.' " Grandfather looked into David's eyes. "Be an eagle, David Livingstone."

A few days later David hurried down Shuttle Row toward the classroom. He saw Neil with a crowd headed for the pub.

"Come go with us," they yelled.

David hesitated. He

GUESS

1. was tempted to go along.
2. didn't know how to say no.
3. joined the crowd.

While David was trying to think of a polite way to say no, the group surrounded him on all sides. One of the rough lads spoke,

GUESS

1. "We think you study too much."
2. "You need not be a teetotaler just because your father is."
3. "You need some fun."

David drew himself up as tall as possible. He listened to them make fun of his father. He planted his feet in the road. In spite of that the crowd pushed him toward the pub.

Finally David yelled, "Stop!

GUESS

1. "You think, do you? Well, I can think, too."
2. "I think study is important."
3. "I'm not going to the pub. I'm not!"

David glared at the crowd. "I don't need anyone to think for me. I can think for myself."

Slowly the group pulled away.

"Leave him alone! We don't need—"

The crowd moved on, cursing. Only Neil stopped and looked back.

"You'll never have any friends now, David."

4

A New Day

When David joined the church in Hamilton, he said,

<table>
<tr><td>GUESS</td><td>1. "The world looks different when you are saved."
2. "It's like I was color-blind, but now I can see."
3. "The church is a good place."</td></tr>
</table>

David compared not believing in Christ to being color-blind. He said, "Now I can see."

His Bible teacher, Mr. David Hogg, held his hand and said, "Now, David, make religion the every day business of your life. Temptation will get the best of you if you have fits and starts."

Grandfather wept. "I can go to heaven now, knowing you believe in Christ."

David joined the church

<table>
<tr><td>GUESS</td><td>1. because of his family.
2. to prove he was a man.
3. because he believed in Jesus and wanted to learn more.</td></tr>
</table>

Pastor Moir loaned David a book, *Journey to Lattakoo*. David could picture Johnney Campbell, a missionary to Africa, sitting in an ox wagon under his yellow umbrella telling the natives of Jesus. He read everything he could find about missionaries and listened to the church people say,

1. "The day of opportunity is here."
2. "The ones who know the gospel should go tell the heathen."
3. "But who will go?"

David heard all those things and realized someone must go tell the good news of salvation. He read of Dr. Charles Gutzlaff, who not only brought healing to people's souls but also healed their bodies. *Now, that is a good idea,* David thought.

As he tended his machines in the mill, he seemed to hear Dr. Gutzlaff saying,

GUESS

1. "Send medical help to China."
2. "Send doctors who know Jesus."
3. "Send doctors. Send doctors."

All those words seemed to blend into the rumble of the machinery. David could not study; he could only think of missions. He seemed to hear the verse "The harvest truly is plenteous, but the labourers are few." Then, "Who will go? Who will go? Who will go?"

Aloud he cried, "Here am I, Lord, send me." The rumble of the machinery swallowed his words. David felt

GUESS

1. God was calling him.
2. he was dreaming.
3. he was sick.

When David told Grandfather, "I feel God is calling me to missions," they rejoiced together.

Grandfather said,

GUESS

1. "It's too bad there is no money for missionary training."
2. "You will have to stay in the mill."
3. "We will find a way together."

Grandfather told David, "I've saved all the money paid by the geological society for samples since you have been collecting. If you save all the money you make from four years in the mill, you can go to college."

"What of the family expense?" asked David.

"Both Agnes and Janet are now working, so your mother agrees to save your salary."

David said,

GUESS

1. "Four years is too long to work and wait."
2. "When God called, He already had a way."
3. "I think someone should pay for me to go to college."

David thought it was worth any price to answer God's call. He worked four years and studied the books to prepare himself for college work. He did this because

GUESS

1. his father made him.
2. he wanted to glorify God.
3. he thought it easy.

Though it wasn't easy, David wanted to glorify God. He also wanted to learn self-control. When he wanted to say angry words, he asked himself, *Would these words glorify God?* When he felt like fighting, he stopped himself and gave a soft answer. When he felt like telling a lie, he said, "Speak the truth and lie not."

In 1836 David registered at Anderson College in Glasgow after walking eight miles from Blantyre. Everything seemed elegant to

37

David: the carpet, carvings, wooden panels on the walls, and even brass doorknobs.

Another student, James Young, told David about a boarding house. Together they walked through a neighborhood called Dodge City. It was called that because

GUESS	1. pigeons flew everywhere.
	2. pigeon droppings fell freely.
	3. cowboys rode horses there.

David didn't dodge quickly enough. "Ugly pigeons," he said.

At the boarding house, James Young introduced his roommate, William Thomson.

"Just call me Will," he said.

Together they entered the old fashioned dining room. "This is Lyon Playfair, another first year medical student, and Mums McCoy, our landlady. Lyon found out about Dodge City today, the same way you did."

David liked the lads. They teased and joked with each other. David enjoyed the good will. The three students told Mums McCoy,

GUESS	1. "Please let David stay here with us."
	2. "Forget about David."
	3. "He is only a mill lint-head."

David knew that cotton lint covered the workers' hair when they came out of the mill, and he didn't like being called a lint-head. But David was happy when James, Lyon, and Will all begged Mums McCoy to let him stay.

Lyon was his roommate. Already he felt they were friends. Lyon said,

GUESS	1. "We can't work all the time."
	2. "I see we are going to have to teach you to play."
	3. "You've had enough of work."

Lyon felt all work and no play wouldn't do. He said, "I see we will have to teach you to play."

"Oh, no, I want to learn everything about medicine. I won't have time for drinking and such," David answered.

"That's not what I mean. Let's set aside Wednesday afternoons for exploring around Glasgow. We can ride horses, sail in the bay, or just tramp the hills. Come, be my friend, David Livingstone." Lyon held out his hand with a smile.

David smiled back. All four young men became fast friends.

Later, David explained his new address to the college clerk. "On my registration, put my roommates as Lyon Playfair and William Thomson."

"Oh, you mean their Lordships Playfair and Thomson?" the clerk asked.

David gulped. "I didn't know they were lords from England. I only know they are my good friends."

5

Success and Failure

During David's two years at Anderson College, he learned the ways of polished gentlemen. Polished gentlemen have

GUESS

1. good manners.
2. kind words.
3. understanding and helpfulness.

David found that actions glorifying God were considered polished by his friends.

Wednesdays proved to be his favorite day. He and Lyon explored Loch Lomond and the wooded hills of the Trussacks. They even went ten miles off the mainland to see Ailsa Craig* rising 1,000 feet from the water.

David wanted to see everything, learn everything, do everything. When he brought home high marks and good reports, Father said,

1. "Well done, Son."

*A rock.

GUESS

2. "I wish I could show this to Grandfather."

3. "Perhaps Grandfather sees from heaven."

David choked when he remembered Grandfather's saying, "I can go to heaven now, knowing you are a believer in Christ." Grandfather's death hurt David because Grandfather

GUESS

1. loved him.

2. loaned him books.

3. helped him plan for college.

Grandfather did all that and more. He glorified God.

Before the end of David's second year at college, he ran out of money. Now, he knew he must

GUESS

1. quit school.

2. steal.

3. pray for a loan.

David prayed to God for an answer, so when his brother John said, "Oh, David, if you are ever short of money, my wife and I can lend you some," David gulped down his pride and said,

GUESS

1. "I'll pay you back."

2. "No, I can't accept charity."

3. "I'm too proud to borrow."

"I'll pay you back, John, soon as school is out. I'll work in the mill, honest I will."

So after great successes, on the last Friday after school, David went home and returned to the mill the next Monday morning.

When Neil saw him, he laughed. "I see yer back in the mill with us. All that fancy schooling fer nothing. Ye could have been having fun at the pub."

42

As soon as possible, David repaid his brother. He also talked to Pastor Moir.

"Isn't there some way I can get to China? I know I haven't finished my studies, but I'll be an old man by that time the way things are going."

"There is a way, David. If you would write to the London Missionary Society, they could pay for your training and send you to the field. Once on the field you would receive a regular salary."

"How can they do that?"

"People who love God and want to help missions send money to them," the pastor said. "They accept only all rounders to send as missionaries."

"What do you mean, 'all rounders'?" David asked.

"They try to send people with mechanical skills or medical skills—people like yourself—who can do something besides preach. A missionary does a million things besides preach."

"Then they might accept the likes of me," David said. "I want to be a medical missionary."

David sent them a letter.

In August 1838, David received a reply. "We, the directors of the London Missionary Society, request your presence 13 August in London for an interview and examination."

David thought the letter showed him

GUESS	1. God's will for his life.
	2. a trick of the devil to make him quit the mill.
	3. that he could never pass the examination.

Since David wanted to follow God's will for his life, he went to Mrs. Sewall's boarding home for missionary candidates at 57 Aldersgate in London. His roommate was Joseph Moore from the south of England.

"Oh, I say, old man, we are here for the same tests on Monday. But let us see jolly old London town on Tuesday, while our tests are being corrected," Joseph Moore suggested.

David agreed. He liked Joseph because

1. he had shoulders like an ox.

| GUESS |

2. they were so different.
3. they had the same goal—to glorify God.

Though they were different, they had the same goals. After Monday's tests, they fell into bed. They were too tired to talk of tomorrow's sight-seeing.

David always remembered that Tuesday and seeing the tall buildings—some five stories high—the crowds, and the smokey air. But the most important thing he remembered was

| GUESS |

1. the tower of London.
2. St. Pauls, the beautiful church of London.
3. the London Bridge, which took eighty years to rebuild.
4. Westminster Abbey, founded in 1065.

"What beauty!" David's neck was stiff from gazing at the Gothic vaulting, the arches, and the rose window of Westminster Abbey. He gazed at the rows of monuments and memorials to great statesmen, scientists, and philosophers, and the graves of the past kings and queens of England.

If someone had told David he would some day be buried there, he would have

| GUESS |

1. scoffed at the idea.
2. been happy.
3. laughed.

He would not have believed such a thing.

Back at 57 Aldersgate, the boys learned the good news. Joseph received ninety on his written exam and David a ninety-five. "Hallelujah!" they told each other.

Joseph said, "Pray, pray, pray we will do as well on the oral exams and the interview."

David added, "You know we go home if we don't pass."

Wednesday morning while David was answering seventeen questions aloud, he

<table>
<tr><td rowspan="3">GUESS</td><td>1. grew warmer and warmer.</td></tr>
<tr><td>2. felt beads of sweat roll down his chest.</td></tr>
<tr><td>3. gave an answer to every question.</td></tr>
</table>

He hoped the answers he gave were correct. He couldn't tell by the expression on the face of Mr. Prentice, who only scratched in his little book with a quill pen.

After lunch, Mr. Prentice said, "You lads both passed and will be interviewed now. David, come with me, and Joseph, go with Mr. Willis."

David followed Mr. Prentice to a small bedroom that served as an office during the day.

Mr. Prentice smiled. "Master Livingstone, you've done yourself proud. You've shown you are resolved to glorify God, and we are here to help you."

Mr. Prentice told David of some of the hardships and suffering on the mission field. He was trying to

<table>
<tr><td rowspan="3">GUESS</td><td>1. discourage David.</td></tr>
<tr><td>2. enlighten David.</td></tr>
<tr><td>3. test David's resolve to go.</td></tr>
</table>

Mr. Prentice was testing David's resolve and dedication. "Now I want to ask what you would do if everything were to go wrong on the mission field and you were the only one left to carry on the work."

David swallowed, then gulped for air. "Though everyone else be dead and I myself sick, I would still go on, and if I failed, I would at least die in the field."

Mr. Prentice stood up, shook David's hand, and wept. "I believe you would, David Livingstone. I believe you would!"

Mr. Prentice explained, "Your next step in the process of being accepted for missionary work is a training session. You and Joseph will go to Ongar. You are to learn how to work with foreign languages, study the Bible, and learn how to preach."

The three months passed quickly. The lads stayed in the home of Reverend Richard Cecil, who was especially good at languages. He showed them how to take a strange word in any language, listen to the sounds, and spell it. He showed them how words are put together in many languages.

They also studied the Bible, but Mr. Cecil was a busy man. When it came to sermons, he simply told them to write one every week. "Before you leave, I'll arrange for you to preach your best sermon to a congregation."

That was their downfall! When Joseph tried to preach, he

GUESS

1. stumbled over his words.
2. forgot the first word of every paragraph.
3. read his sermon.

Joseph forgot the first word of each paragraph.
David did worse. He

GUESS

1. stuttered.
2. opened his mouth, but no words came out.
3. ran away.

When David faced the people, he remembered that day when he and Jeremy laughed in church. He remembered the scowls, the sour disapproving faces, the terror. He opened his mouth and said, "I have forgotten it all." He hurried out of the church.

Naturally, Mr. Cecil could not give a good report to the London Missionary Society.

"I'm a failure! I'm a failure!" despaired David when they returned to 57 Aldersgate.

"I'm as bad," Joseph wailed.

"No, not as bad. You didn't run away."

David could

1. go home and work in the mill.

2. go back for another three months with Pastor Cecil.

3. work in London.

David and Joseph went back to Mr. Cecil and repeated their training. They learned to preach in front of people and were such good friends that everyone called them David and Jonathan, after the Bible characters.

6

The Mission Field

Back in London, Joseph Moore went to Chesnut College, near his home, while David stayed in London as a student. Mr. Prentice said, "We are proud you lads went back and took your training over again. 'Tis hard to repeat but sometimes necessary."

David agreed because

| GUESS |

1. he really needed more practice preaching.
2. now Mr. Prentice was pleased.
3. he had more time with his friend.

David was thankful for the extra practice preaching. "I needed it," he admitted. Now that he was accepted by the London Missionary Society, he was anxious to get to the mission field.

So was his new roommate at 57 Aldersgate, D.G. Watt.

"You don't have a first name—just D.G.?" David asked.

"As a matter of fact, I do—'David'—like you; but there were too many Davids in the family, so I got D.G."

"What is your mission field?"

"Oh, I planned to go to China, but no missionaries are allowed in during the Opium War. I was told to consider the West Indies, Africa, or India."

"What!" David exclaimed, "I didn't know! I, too, am planning to go to China."

David bounded down the stairs to Dr. Prentice's little office. He said,

1. "Why didn't you tell me of the Opium War?"
2. "Won't they allow a few missionaries into the country?"
3. "It isn't fair. I've been studying all about China for so long."

David didn't have to say anything. Mr. Prentice saw his stormy face and apologized. "We are sorry about the news that came today. The Chinese government is firm. Please consider other fields in God's great universe."

On May 5, 1839, David wrote to Janet. "I must have a willing mind to know God's will for me. It seems the door to China is closed. Pray God will open another door."

David made many new friends in London. On the mission field, it is good to have friends at home because

1. they will pray for you.
2. they will send you money and supplies.
3. they can tell people about your work.

The most important thing friends at home can do is to pray, even when they don't know the missionary's troubles.

David prayed, but he also learned from his friends. Dr. Risdon Bennett invited him to Charing Cross Hospital to practice treating the sick.

Dr. George Wilson showed him his collections of plants and rocks.

Professor Richard Owen made David promise to bring back any unusual bone formations he found.

At mealtime, David and D.G. told each other everything they had discovered. At one of Mrs. Sewall's dinners, David asked, "Who is that long-bearded man sitting at the next table?"

"Dr. Robert Moffatt, the missionary from Africa. He lectures and recruits new missionaries."

"I believe I can recognize a man when I see one. I'd like to hear him speak," David responded.

Soon David tagged behind Dr. Moffat to every lecture. He prayed and prayed for God to show him what to do.

"From my home in Kuruman, I can look to the north and see the smoke of a thousand villages—villages where the name of Christ has never been uttered," Dr. Moffat lectured.

Finally David spoke to the missionary privately. He asked,

GUESS	1. "Do you think black men would like me?"
	2. "What kind of weather do they have?"
	3. "Do you think I would do for Africa?"

Dr. Moffat answered, "I believe you would do for Africa if you are willing to go inside the continent. The coast has been explored, but maps have an empty space marked 'Unknown' north of our station. That is where workers are needed. Would you dare go to the unknown?"

David looked at the map of Africa. He laid his finger on the spot marked Unknown. "What is the use of waiting for the end of this abominable Opium War? I will go at once to Africa."

Dr. Prentice was delighted. "Now that you know God's will, you must finish your studies here, then get your diploma from the medical and surgical department of Anderson College."

David agreed; he

GUESS	1. knew he needed his medical diploma.
	2. was pleased to be able to see his family again.
	3. wanted to work in the mill.

David was pleased to go home before leaving for Africa. He wanted to tell everyone good-bye.

Joseph Moore came to visit him before he left. Together they went to Exeter Hall to hear Prince Albert, Queen Victoria's new husband, make his first speech. David heard the prince say, "You made a law years ago to stop the slave trade in Africa, but it has never stopped." David vowed he would do something about that.

In November 1840, David

GUESS	1. said good-bye to his family.
	2. visited the mill.
	3. sailed for Africa.

David embarked on the steamship *George*.

Every passenger but David was seasick. "How come you are not sick?" moaned William Ross, a fellow missionary. "You've never been on the sea before."

David answered, "The only reason I can think of is that I walked on the swinging bridge over the River Clyde. It felt just like walking on this deck. It lurched and swayed at every step."

"You're lucky," William murmured, as he headed for the rail of the ship, feeling sick again.

That night David wrote D.G. a letter telling him of the trip. He said, "I wasn't seasick because of an experience I had as a child. I wonder what other childhood experiences will come in handy now that I'm grown."

He didn't tell D.G. about the teasing he got because he was not married. Instead he wrote, "Captain Donaldson taught me enough astronomy to be able to navigate a boat. He showed me how to use the quadrant, frequently sitting up past midnight to take lunar observations." A missionary needs to know that because

GUESS	1. it is easy to get lost.
	2. the stars are important.
	3. finding the way in the jungle is difficult.

And all that is true.

The trip took fourteen months, giving David time to learn the rudiments of the Bechuana language from the New Testament and dictionary given him by Dr. Moffat. A Dutchman was aboard ship, so David learned his language also. He wrote Reverend Cecil, "Thanks to your training in sounding words, I find it fairly easy.

Your teaching goes with me, dear brother."

The ship docked for repairs in Cape Town, South Africa. Since David longed to see a mission station, he walked to the nearest one.

"I'm afraid we are not prepared for visitors," the pastor's wife apologized. "My husband and child are very sick, and I don't know what to do."

David said,

GUESS

1. "God has sent a visitor."
2. "God has sent a doctor."
3. "God has sent a plumber."

While David tended the sick, he looked over the mission compound. He saw

GUESS

1. a mud fence surrounding the place.
2. a mud-plastered chapel.
3. straw huts for natives.
4. a schoolroom with a straw roof.

David saw all those and the missionaries' home. The verandas on all four sides held many chairs. He sat there and fanned himself while listening to the breathing of his patients. He preached to rows of natives wrapped in bright colored cloth, while the pastor's wife interpreted his words.

It seemed

GUESS

1. good to be a missionary at last.
2. frightening.
3. strange.

David felt like a missionary for the first time, but as soon as the pastor and child were well, he hurried to the Cape, praying the ship had not left without him.

It was still in port but preparations were underway to sail to Port Elizabeth.

Back on board, David wrote to his father. "I visited a real mission station and was much gratified to talk with a pastor about the work among the natives. I saw my first missionary converts and my expectations have been far exceeded. Everything I witnessed surpassed my hope."

By July 7, 1841, David had left the ship at Port Elizabeth and hired an ox wagon for the ten-week trip inland to Kuruman, Robert Moffat's mission station.

He also hired ten natives and fourteen oxen.

"Fourteen oxen? Whatever for? How can we need that many for one wagon?" David demanded in disbelief.

"You will see, Master David Livingstone," the equipment manager said. "Remember you are going five hundred twenty miles. I will tell the natives to take you there. They only speak Bechuana, but they are trustworthy, at least until you pay them. So do not pay until you reach Kuruman. You understand?"

David nodded his head, climbed into the wagon, and they rolled northward.

As David listened to the natives speak, he

GUESS

1. gave orders in Bechuana.
2. was quiet and listened for many days.
3. paid no attention to what they said.

It was difficult for David to understand the jabbering of the natives. "Are these the words I studied in the New Testament and the dictionary? They sound so different." He decided not to speak until he could make sense to the natives.

Several days passed. They covered twenty miles a day by traveling morning and evening. The afternoons were too hot for travel but not for mosquitoes and tsetse flies.

When an ox died during the night, David was concerned and wanted to know why. He pointed to the dead ox and said in English, "Why? Why?" knowing the natives did not understand English.

They found a dead tsetse fly, put him on the oxen, and gnashed their teeth.

David knew then that the ox died because of the fly's bite.

54

As the days went on David understood more and more of the native language. One day he overheard the men talking about him. "What a weakling. He rides in the wagon while we walk." He saw them pointing and snickering behind their hands.

Oh, ho, thought David, *they don't know I walked twenty miles a day in the mill. 'Tis true, I shouldn't expect them to do what I cannot do.*

The next morning David took his place at the head of the caravan. He set a good pace—not too fast, not too slow. They rested at noon, and David set out again. Plod, plod he went, trudge, trudge, trudge. The green of the coast disappeared, and dry brown grass took its place.

By the end of the third hot day,

GUESS

1. the natives were dragging.
2. the natives begged to go slower.
3. the natives stopped.

The respect in their voices told David he had changed in their eyes from a weakling to a leader.

55

7
Lions

"**W**elcome to Kuruman," Robert Hamilton cried. "We have been expecting you. How was the trip?"

David introduced himself to Hamilton and to Mr. and Mrs. Roger Edwards. "The trip was so pleasant that I never tired of it. We lost four oxen, though."

"You were lucky; sometimes all fourteen die. Then you have trouble," Roger Edwards replied.

"You will be sleeping in Mary's room. I hope you don't mind." Mrs. Edwards directed the porters to take David's baggage.

"Who is Mary?" David asked.

"Dr. Moffat's daughter. You didn't meet her in London?"

"No, I just met the doctor and his wife. I didn't know there were children."

"Two girls," Mrs. Edwards went on. "Mary is the older. She has been writing to a seminary student. Did she get married?"

"Nobody said anything about it." David could see Mrs. Edwards was disappointed that he knew nothing.

"When are they coming home?" David questioned.

"We don't know. There have been delays, always delays." Mrs. Edwards sighed as she left David to clean up.

The thing that impressed David most about the mission station was

GUESS	1. the church with hand-sanded pews.
	2. the classrooms for all ages.
	3. the "eye of Kuruman."

The "eye of Kuruman" was a fountain that poured out four million gallons of water a day. Irrigation of the orchard and fields produced food enough for all. A lovely garden with stone walkways, trimmed hedges, and a multitude of flowers was made possible by this life-giving water. Truly it was an oasis in the surrounding dry desert.

"A place to rest and talk with God. Truly my cup runneth over," David mused.

Sleeping in Mary's room made him wonder about her. He couldn't help but appreciate the clean, embroidered sheets and pillow cases with many little pink roses. *She must love roses,* he thought.

David's orders were to wait for Dr. Moffat, but as days dragged by he became restless.

He decided

GUESS	1. to sing to the natives.
	2. to teach school.
	3. to go live in a native village.

"I'm going to live with the natives," David announced one morning.

"Never heard of a missionary doing that." Mr. Edwards sniffed.

"Well, Dr. Gutslaff did it in China. I'm going to the village to the north. The one whose smoke we can see," David insisted.

"I've been to a few villages, but practically no one comes to hear me preach." Mr. Edwards scowled.

"Oh, you know the language?" David questioned.

"No, one of the natives interprets for me."

"Well, I've been studying for months. Maybe I'll be able to communicate with the natives," David said.

"Don't count on it," was all Mr. Edwards had to say.

"Me David. You _____?"

David felt like a missionary as he approached the native village. As he walked along the dusty path, children ran out to see him. Most of them had never seen a white man.

David sat down on a rock and pointed to himself. "David." He said it three times, and finally one little girl whispered bashfully, "David?"

David gave her a gift. Now everyone wanted to say, "David, David, David." Their cries rang out. David gave them all trinkets. The most popular was a tiny mirror.

Next David pointed to one child. Back and forth he pointed, "David, you?" Finally, the child gave his name, "Nambe." David said, "David," pointing to himself, then, "Nambe," pointing to the child.

All the children eventually gave their names, and David repeated every child's name before he would say the next new name. Over and over David struggled not to forget one single person. Each time he said the name, he looked into the brown eyes of the child and smiled. Since his own eyes were brown, David thought he had one thing in common with them.

Later the children

<table>
<tr><td rowspan="3">GUESS</td><td>1. introduced him to their mothers and fathers.</td></tr>
<tr><td>2. invited him to lunch.</td></tr>
<tr><td>3. gave him a mat on which to sleep.</td></tr>
</table>

The children took good care of him. By listening carefully and making a game of the language, he slowly learned. The children were excited to be teachers and delighted in his progress. Little did they know that the scratches he made on paper were a sound dictionary that spelled the words the way they sounded.

In time David learned the habits, thoughts, and laws of the Bakwains. He obeyed their rules and respected their strange ways. He helped the medicine man get healing juices from plants and showed him how to use them. In a short time, the Bakwains were his friends.

Since the Moffats were still in London, David and Mr. Edwards decided to explore.

"We need to find a good place for a new mission station. When the Moffats come back, we won't be needed here," Mr. Edwards pointed out.

Their journey took them 700 miles. Vegetation grew in clumps in the pale soft sand. David showed Mr. Edwards a plant that the natives had pointed out to him. This plant had a tuber* deep under the hot sand. The tuber, which contained a cool fluid, was as large as a child's head.

"I would never have expected to find water here," Mr. Edwards marveled.

"They tell me there are tracts of what must be watermelons," David added. In time they found these also. Along the way, David drew maps and collected samples. He

GUESS	1. collected rocks.
	2. collected grasses and flowers.
	3. preached to the natives.

Besides collecting, David led prayer meetings.

Mr. Edwards had to admit that the natives listened to David, though he struggled with his words. David thought trying to speak was better than using the interpreter.

They found the ideal spot for a mission station 250 miles to the north. Both David and Mr. Edwards agreed it was a place where God could be glorified. The natives were friendly and said they would help. The natives called the area *Mabotsa*.

When they returned to Kuruman, David held a prayer meeting for the workers who lived in the compound. Mebalwe believed in Christ. His joy was so great that he said he would serve David the rest of his life.

David said,

GUESS	1. "Don't serve me, serve Jesus."
	2. "You must think of yourself first."
	3. "I don't preach to make a slave of you."

*A potato-like root.

David wanted the native to serve Jesus.

Mebalwe and David made two more explorations to the north, preaching and making maps as they went. Everywhere David told how wrong slavery was. "Do not sell more natives to the white man for money," he would say.

Mebalwe helped collect samples of vegetation and rocks. He thought it was a game. If David could find no record of a plant or stone, he simply made up Latin names himself.

In London these samples

GUESS	1. were ignored.
	2. caused great excitement.
	3. were worthless.

It was much later that David learned of the terrific excitement caused by his samples.

Finally, in June 1843, David's letters were answered, and he got his orders from the London Missionary Society to form a new station. With the orders came several ox wagons filled with supplies, so Mr. and Mrs. Edwards, along with David, set out for Mabotsa.

The Bakatlas tribe welcomed them. Boba, the medicine man, was especially delighted to see David again.

Since David could speak the language, he was able to enlist men from the village to help with building a station. They soon learned to

GUESS	1. make bricks from clay.
	2. make round buildings.
	3. make square buildings.

"Easy to build round buildings," they insisted. All native huts were round, even the meeting house. David was inclined to let the buildings be round, but Mrs. Edwards objected.

"How can I place the furniture against the walls if they curve? The room would look terrible. I won't have it!"

That meant that David, Mr. Edwards, and Mebalwe were the

only bricklayers. No one else could think in straight lines. The work was heavy, but that wasn't the greatest problem. The greatest problem was

GUESS
1. bees.
2. flies.
3. lions.

At first, lions came at night, killing a few cattle. Later, they came in broad daylight. Everyone knew that people would be killed once the cattle were gone. The missionaries prayed. The chief asked David to attend a council meeting.

"The truth is that if we kill one lion, the rest will never come back," the chief explained.

"Then we must kill at least one!" David agreed.

"Will you join us?" asked the chief.

David

GUESS
1. agreed.
2. admitted it was too dangerous for a missionary.
3. said he would pray for them.

That night they formed a circle. David and Mebalwe had guns; the others held spears. Everyone was silent and serious as the moon went in and out behind the clouds.

Slowly the lions crept toward the cattle pens. Several leaped and downed a cow. After their feast, the lions turned and saw the ring of men. They charged. David fired at thirty yards. When he reached down to reload his gun, he heard a warning shout.

In an instant a lion seized him by the shoulder. Growling horribly close to his ear, he shook David as a dog shakes a rat.

The remaining lions broke through the circle. Natives fled, shouting and screaming. David felt a stupor, a sort of dreaminess, come over him. He had no sense of pain or feeling of terror. He just trusted the Lord.

Then Mebalwe shot into the air. The lion dropped David and sprang at Mebalwe, wounding him slightly. The chief screamed

and waved his spear. The lion

GUESS

1. prepared to spring upon the chief.
2. fell dead at the feet of the chief.
3. succumbed to David's bullet.

The chief gazed at the dead lion and shook violently.

Natives carried David to the chief's hut and bathed his arm. David directed Boba to apply antiseptic, straighten the arm bone, put in a screw to secure the three splintered parts, and to piece the bone from the shoulder socket to make a false joint. David also

GUESS

1. watched the medicine man sew eleven places where the lion had torn his flesh.
2. took some medicine.
3. slept for two days.

The village was safe once again. After all that, David fainted.

8

Romance

Because of his injury, David could no longer help with the build-ing. He returned to Kuruman on horseback. As he galloped into the compound, David heard natives chanting, "The Moffats are coming, the Moffats are coming."

Hamilton grinned. "You are just in time. Everything is ready."

"I'm going to meet them," David stated. "I can't wait any longer."

"Go, if you must," Hamilton agreed. "I'm glad your shoulder is better. I understand you had a bad time these last months."

David didn't stop for a coat or hat. Since spring arrived, he felt better. The pain in his shoulder was less now, and he was rested. The desert

GUESS

1. was green for a change.
2. bloomed with flowers.
3. was covered with water.

After he had traveled through greenery and flowers for fifteen miles, David could see the ox wagons in the distance. *Will there be two girls or only one?* David wondered why his heart beat so fast. "Come on, Dobbin!" he said to his horse.

"Livingstone," Moffat called, "why so fast? This isn't Ascot or the Derby. I say, how are you?"

"Fine, fine." David held out his good hand. His eyes darted from Mrs. Moffat to the eager girls, who leaned forward. *Two girls; then Mary didn't marry that preacher,* he thought with satisfaction.

"Tie your horse to the back of the wagon and come sit with us," invited Mrs. Moffat.

David sat with them. He

GUESS	1. talked to Mr. Moffatt.
	2. talked to the girls.
	3. talked to Mary.

David told everyone of his adventures.

When the wagon was safely within the mission compound and everyone was rushing about, David asked Mary to walk in the garden.

"I always loved the eye of Kuruman." Mary smiled. "It gives life to so many things."

Mary didn't look like the girl David had imagined. She was a beautiful woman. *She's all I want,* he thought.

"You're going to have some explaining to do to Mrs. Edwards, I fear. She thought you would stay in London as a clergyman's wife."

Mary blushed. "I did, too."

"Why didn't you?" David was puzzled.

"Did you ever meet anyone who was perfect? Wilbur was such. If you don't believe me, ask him!" Mary stopped.

"Then why didn't you marry the perfect gentleman?"

"Because, David, I could not love him. I tried to force myself. I prayed and prayed God would give me a proper love. But I could not bear to kiss him. I only wanted to get away and come home to my beloved Africa."

"You like it here? You like mission work?" David questioned.

"Indeed, I do. I love the natives. I love teaching. I belong here, not sipping tea in a London parlor," Mary answered.

David whispered, "Thank You, God."

David was thankful because

GUESS	1. he thought God had saved Mary for him.
	2. he hated Wilbur.
	3. he thought Mary was a good teacher.

He believed that God had saved Mary for him.

In the months to come, David's shoulder healed. It wasn't as strong as before, and he could only raise his arm as high as his neck. But it was a wonder he could use it at all.

David spent every possible moment with Mary. She resumed her teaching, and David listened outside the schoolroom door. He was always eager to walk home with her.

Together they worked on the samples. Mary often made little drawings of the complete plant to be sent with the pressed leaves, flowers, or twigs.

"What does this whitish streak mean in this rock?" she would ask David, who loved to explain things.

He loved to tell her of Scotland. "You would find it hard to believe the beauty we see every morning looking over the Firth of Clyde up the green hillsides to the towering trees and the wispy clouds, drifting in the vast sky."

"I'd love to see it," Mary murmured.

"May I take you there one day?" David looked into her brown eyes and felt he could see her soul—so pure, so honest, so trusting. "Oh, Mary, will you be my wife? I know I'm not perfect, like Wilbur, but I do love you. I believe God saved you for me."

He kissed her, and the promise was given.

"I couldn't love you if you were perfect," Mary said.

The family gave their blessing to the engagement. They could talk of nothing but the wedding.

David felt uncomfortable because

GUESS	1. he was weak.
	2. he didn't know anything about weddings.
	3. he knew the house at Mabotsa wasn't even started.

David said good-bye to Mary. "We've been building castles in the air, but now it's time I got back to Mabotsa and built a solid house on the ground."

He wrote to D.G., "Let Moore, dear good fellow, know of my coming marriage. It will comfort all your hearts to know that I am become as great a fool as any of you ... in love! Words, yea thoughts, fail, so I leave it to your imagination. She's my Mary; she's all I want."

To the London Missionary Society, he wrote: "It was not without much serious consideration and earnest prayer that I became engaged to Mary Moffat. I hope this has your approval."

Though David's arm was not completely healed, he rode back to Mabotsa. He dreamed of Mary and their new home as he rode the 250 miles.

When David arrived, he found that Mr. and Mrs. Edwards' home was finished. "I guess I'll have to be satisfied," Mrs. Edwards moaned. David noticed that

GUESS	1. the roof was crooked.
	2. the windows would not open or close.
	3. the door hung crooked.

David was not a carpenter any more than Mr. Edwards, but he had taken geometry. "I'll have to be careful with my house, because a beautiful new bride doesn't deserve a crooked house," he remarked.

"You mean you're getting married to Mary Moffat?" Mrs. Edwards was thunderstruck with the news. "You're bringing her here. Oh, she's a smart one, she is; knows how to do everything in a mission field. You did well to win her, David. Somehow, I always thought she'd do better than you."

David's feelings were hurt, but

GUESS	1. he knew Mary chose him over the perfect Wilbur.
	2. he thought Mrs. Edwards was flighty.
	3. he didn't care.

68

David told Mebalwe all about his romance with Mary. "Mebalwe, she could have married a perfect man, lived in London, had every lovely thing in the world. But she came back to Africa, and she loves me." David felt better for saying it.

They started the house. David drew all the plans before they began.

"It will be fifty-two feet by twenty feet. We'll start at the bottom with stone, and if that gets too heavy, we'll finish with brick."

David wrote to Mary, "It is pretty hard work. Almost enough to drive love out of my head; but my love is not in my head, it is in my heart and won't come out. You are as dear to me as ever, and will be as long as our lives are spared."

In September 1844, David wrote, "The time of separation is becoming beautifully less," and signed the letter, "Your most affectionate and confident lover, D. Livingstone."

Four months later, he went back to Kuruman to claim his bride. With the house finished, the chapel complete, and one small schoolroom built, he felt their married life could begin.

Mr. and Mrs. Edwards went with him, but he asked Mebalwe to be his best man.

Mrs. Moffat arranged

GUESS	1. wedding music.
	2. beautiful flowers.
	3. green gowns for the bridesmaids.
	4. a large decorated wedding cake.

All those things were wonderful, but the bride's gown, sent by an aunt in Paris, outdid everything else. David was overcome.

None of that mattered when he saw his bride, all in white, floating down the aisle on the arm of Dr. Robert Moffat. The old Kuruman mission faded from view—nothing counted but Mary. David trembled, his forehead was wet. He could hardly speak his vows. But when he kissed Mary, David knew God was pleased, and he was satisfied.

9

Laughter and Tears

David's new house rang with laughter. Mary made all the difference. "All my life I've been working, studying, striving. I always feel the need to press onward," David told Mary.

"Well, now, dear husband, it is time for play," Mary answered.

Later he wrote to his friend, Lyon, "You always tried to teach me the value of play. Now I know what you mean. Mary has taught me to let my head grow wise but to keep my heart young and playful."

David was happy because he

GUESS	1. preached to the natives.
	2. taught in the school.
	3. had a family.

David had many reasons for happiness. First, baby Robert came to be with them. Then Nannie arrived, and Mary and David rejoiced in their little family.

Occasionally natives from other tribes visited. About two years after David and Mary settled at Mabotsa, a native came from the Bechuana country.

"Sechele, our chief, wants to kill David Livingstone," the native told Mebalwe. When Mebalwe told David, he wanted to know why. "I've done nothing to Sechele. Why would he want to kill me?"

"You didn't go to the Bechuana country when you were looking for a place to put a mission station," Mebalwe explained.

"We made three trips of seven hundred miles or more. How could I go farther?" David demanded.

"You didn't go to Bechuana!"

"True, 'tis only forty miles from here. Let me pray about an expedition. I'll talk to Mary," David replied.

David was in trouble for ignoring an important chief.

Mary encouraged him to go. "I'll be fine with the Edwardses here, and the children to keep me busy. You know you always say you want no enemies among the natives." So David and Mebalwe set out to visit Sechele.

"What if he sends warriors to kill us before we get there?" Mebalwe worried.

"I think it's a bluff," David scoffed. "He just wants to meet us."

"I don't know; their chief's strange sometimes," Mebalwe countered.

When the two entered the village, they found the natives weeping.

"What's wrong?" Mebalwe asked.

"The chief's only child is dying."

"I am a doctor," David stated. "Take me to her."

David found that the little girl's appendix was about to burst. When he took out his surgical knives, the natives looked horrified.

Sechele held his hand. "You kill my child, I kill you!"

David gently answered, "If I don't cut out the bad thing, she *will* die." When he saw that wasn't enough for the chief, he said, "If she dies, I die too. All right?"

The chief relented, and David operated just in time. When the child was better, the chief took David to a friend's house where another child lay ill. David gave her medicine, and the child's fever dropped. Sechele was convinced that David was good.

David risked his life because

1. he wanted the chief to think he was important.

GUESS 2. he wanted the natives to listen to the gospel.

3. he wasn't concerned.

Sechele invited David and Mebalwe to eat with him. After the meal, he sat beside David and asked, "White man, why do you come here?" David told him of the Savior—Jesus Christ—about God, and about heaven and hell.

Chief Sechele said, "You startle me. These words make all my bones to shake. I have no more strength in me. But my forefathers were living at the same time as yours, and how is it that they did not send my people word about these terrible things sooner? They all passed away into darkness without knowing where they were going."

David answered,

GUESS 1. "I'm sorry no one came sooner."

2. "Think about what God is saying to you now."

3. "We had no one who would come."

David continued to preach and read the Scripture to Sechele, begging him to think about his soul *now*. Sechele accepted Christ and asked David to come to Bechuana and build a mission station. "I want all the tribe to be saved," he insisted.

"I'll be happy to talk to the natives if you will call a meeting," David said.

Sechele snorted. "Do you imagine these people will ever believe by your merely talking to them? I can make them do nothing except by thrashing them. If you like, I will call my head man and with our whips we will soon make them all believe together."

David said, "That will only make them pretend to believe."

David taught Sechele much from the Bible. They became good friends, but when David said he must go, Sechele was angry.

"Why you go away?" he asked. "Will God go, too?"

"No," David answered, "God is with you always. Jesus says, 'I will never leave thee, nor forsake thee.' And I promise you, Sechele, I will come back."

David and Mary continued at Mabotsa for several years.

Another child was born to them to make their lives even happier, but always David remembered his promise to Sechele.

Finally, Mary said, "I can see God is calling you to the Bechuana country. The Edwardses can carry on this work. Why don't we move?"

"I was afraid you wouldn't want to face a new tribe and move with no house built and the children so small. Mary, I can't ask that of you." David hesitated.

"You are not asking, David. God is my friend, too. I want Him to be glorified as much as you do. Don't be afraid."

They decided to

GUESS	1. move.
	2. stay at Mabotsa.
	3. move to Kolobeng.

They decided to move to Kolobeng in the Bechuana country.

Chief Sechele was considered a "rain maker" by his people. In the past, he had performed chants and dances to the rain god, and rain had come. Now that he was a Christian and did not believe in a rain god, he refused to chant even when a drought came.

To add to the trouble, it rained all around them. The second year of the drought, the natives again begged Sechele, "Chant, just once! Why can't you make rain just once?"

"I cannot," responded Sechele. "Dr. Livingstone says—"

"That is the trouble. You are blind to see that the rain god is displeased with Dr. Livingstone and his Christianity. Our crops die; our children die; we will die. Why does the white man come to plague us? Ask him to permit one chant, just one little chant."

By the third year, the situation was desperate. The Livingstones themselves were without water, and David told Mary, "I must find a healthful place to take the family. But I cannot leave you and the four children. The natives are so angry, they might harm you. They might even harm the new baby."

"Take us along, David. We can go with you in the ox wagon," Mary begged.

David didn't like the idea but knew of nothing else to do.

He led the ox wagon through the brush, in the hot sun with little water, until the children cried themselves sick. "It's too much. Let's go back," he told Mary.

They

GUESS	1. went back to Kolobeng.
	2. found water.
	3. were hurt by the natives.

They went back to Kolobeng.

Fortunately, the native women found water. They dug deep holes in the sand, put down long reeds, and sucked up water. They put the water in ostrich egg shells, which they brought to Chief Sechele. He shared the water with David.

By that time, the Livingstone children ran and played with the natives. The life of the natives was the only life they knew. "They will grow up thinking and talking like natives. They hardly speak English now and are nothing but skin and bones." Mary cried.

"If I only could find a healthful place with water, I could build a new compound like Kuruman," David said.

"Let's try again," Mary urged. "I can see the fierce looks these natives give us. They blame us for all their troubles."

"Yes, they do, and I fear for our lives. We must try once more to find a better place."

Mary and David prepared for another trip. They took more supplies and left while it was still dark. Chief Sechele gave them all the water he could spare.

They traveled a week. Then

GUESS	1. the children became ill.
	2. baby Agnes almost died.
	3. tsetse flies swarmed.

"If a tsetse fly bites one of the children, you know what will happen." Mary worried, seeking to protect them with mosquito netting. "Oh, David, let's go to Kuruman!" Mary finally gave up in despair.

"It's over three hundred miles. Do you think we can make it?" David asked.

In his letters, David never told of the agony of this trip. It must have been one long nightmare. Dust, heat, flies, and mosquitoes were bad enough, but with little water and food, the children suffered terribly.

When they finally pulled into the Kuruman mission compound, Mrs. Moffat greeted them in horror, "Did you not give your wife and children food, David? They are all but dead!"

David must decide to

GUESS	1. give up missionary work.
	2. send Mary and the children back to England.
	3. run away.

Reluctantly, David sent Mary and the children back to England. David wept as he said good-bye. He had taken them all the way to the Cape in South Africa to catch a ship going to England. Delay upon delay kept him from returning to Kuruman.

As David journeyed the one thousand miles back to the north country, he thought of his goals. "Three things I must do to glorify God. First, find a healthful location for a mission. Second, find a passage to the coast, either east or west. Third, do something about this accursed slave trade."

When he finally arrived at Kuruman in September 1852, the people were full of excitement. "Sechele's wife came here and told the news," Mrs. Moffat announced.

"After you left, most of the Bakwains went south," Dr. Moffat explained. "Sechele led the way, but his wife remained with a few others. The Boers* arrived ready for battle."

They came to

GUESS	1. hear the gospel.
	2. kill the Livingstone family.
	3. do a dance.

*White Dutch slave traders.

"When they found you gone, they destroyed your furniture and tore up your books and journals. If your family had been there, you would all be dead," Dr. Moffat continued.

They were angry

GUESS

1. because David spoke against slavery.
2. because David was white.
3. because David sang songs.

"They hate you for opposing slavery and will not let you go north."

David answered slowly, "I will open a path through the north country or perish. I will preach the gospel to the farthest limits of the Barotre country."

Dr. Moffat looked over the desert with tearful eyes. "It may cost you your life, David! I'm warning you!"

10

Discoveries

With determination, David set out northward through the soft, pale sand. On the second week out, he saw a caravan of hunters on a safari. The hunters were

GUESS

1. killing elephants.
2. killing lions.
3. killing tigers.

They were from Europe and killed animals. David hurried forward to greet them. He wanted news from home, and he was lonesome.

As David approached, he realized the hunters recognized him.

"Livingstone, come have dinner with us!" one of the men invited.

How could he refuse? He had lived so long on native food.

After a good dinner and lively conversation, one of the hunters asked, "Livingstone, where are the largest prides of lions? We will give you a thousand dollars to be our guide in the hunt."

"I'm a missionary, not a guide. Thank you for your hospitality, but frankly, I cannot find it in my heart to help you kill helpless animals. I am on my way to find a healthful location for a mission station in the north."

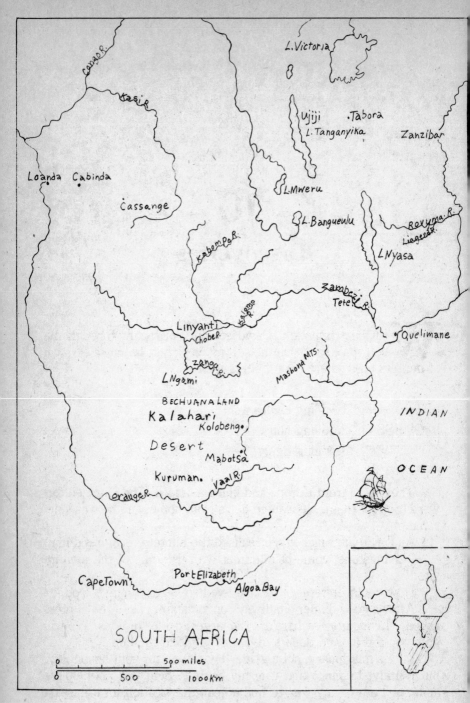

L. Victoria

Congo R.

Kasai R.

Ujiji · Tabora
L. Tanganyika

Zanzibar

Loanda Cabinda

Cassange

L. Mweru

L. Bangueulu

Rovuma R.
Liagenst R.

L. Nyasa

Kabompo R.

Zambesi R.
Tete

Linyanti
Chobe R.

Quelimane

Zanga

L. Ngami

Mashona MTS.

BECHUANALAND

Kalahari
Kolobeng·

INDIAN

Desert
Mabotsa·

Kuruman· Vaal R.

OCEAN

Orange R.

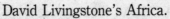

Cape Town   Port Elizabeth
Algoa Bay

SOUTH AFRICA

0   500 miles
0   500   1000 Km

David Livingstone's Africa.

"Others have tried to penetrate those strange lands, Dr. Livingstone. What makes you think you will succeed?"

David answered the hunters,

GUESS	1. "I'm smarter than others."
	2. "I know how to explore."
	3. "God is with me."

David took this opportunity to glorify God. As David said good-bye, Captain Thomas Steele asked, "Have you found anything of interest in your travels?"

"Oh, yes," David answered. "I discovered Lake N'gami. On August first, eighteen forty-nine, my eyes beheld the lake as far as I could see. The natives say it takes three days to go around, so I judge it to be seventy miles." He showed them his maps and the samples of rock, soil, and vegetation he had collected.

Captain Steele said,

GUESS	1. "I had no idea you were doing such detailed scientific work."
	2. "The Royal Geographical Society must know."
	3. "Look at these maps, Oswell!"

Captain Steele went on, "The Royal Geographical Society must know of this find."

"Oh, I send samples of rocks and vegetation to Dr. George Wilson of the Edinburgh Museum," David answered. "Of course, they have to go by ox wagon to the coast and then wait for a ship. It takes months."

"Listen, let us take this information to England. I personally will see that it gets to the Royal Society safely," Captain Steele offered.

After giving Captain Steele his samples and saying good-bye, David went on his way, stopping in native villages.

At night, while David was drawing his maps by firelight, classifying rock and vegetation samples and writing in his journal, the natives

GUESS	1. danced.
	2. chanted.
	3. quarreled.

David wrote to his sister, Agnes, "You never know what childhood experiences will come in handy later. I am able to shut out the noise of the heathen and write in peace because I learned to shut out the noise of the mill."

The next morning, Ramotobi, a young native who had joined David at the last village, remarked, "Soon we see the river."

As the river came into view, David was filled with joy. "Thank God," he cried and named the river *Zambezi*. "Someday I'll explore it to its origin." For now, he was satisfied to examine the area for a possible mission site. It was the dry season, but even now the river's width was three hundred to six hundred yards of flowing water.

"Why are there no native villages here?" David asked Ramotobi.

Ramotobi answered,

GUESS	1. "Too much fever."
	2. "Too many mosquitoes."
	3. "People die here."

"Too much fever. People get sick—die here," Ramotobi said.

While David stood on the bank, the wind increased and blew away hordes of flies and mosquitoes. "I never saw a prettier place," David told Ramotobi. But he turned away in sorrow. "I wonder what causes the fever.

"We will go on." He took one last look at the trees, the plants, and the wild fruits. David always looked for something that could be sold by the natives. "If they go on selling ivory the way they do now, there will soon be no elephants."

David, his mind on other things, followed Ramotobi. Suddenly, Ramotobi cried out, "Look, Master Livingstone, look!"

There was a

| GUESS |

1. lion.
2. tiger.
3. rhinoceros.

From nowhere, a rhinoceros charged at David. Over the river bank and down the path he dashed. Coming up to David, he suddenly stopped. David stared into his eyes. He fought between fear and trust in God. Trust won. David's eyes were peaceful as he stared into those enormous red eyes. Slowly the rhino's eyes became peaceful too, and he walked away.

David quickly joined Ramotobi in a nearby tree.

"How did you do that?" Ramotobi cried.

"I don't know. It was just like the time I slipped while carving my name on a wall. The Scripture flashed before me, 'What time I am afraid, I will trust in thee.' Trust took the place of fear."

"But how did the rhino know it?" Ramotobi asked.

David answered,

| GUESS |

1. "The sight of a white man astonished him."
2. "He saw I wasn't afraid and backed down."
3. "I don't honestly know.

David puzzled with the question for some time but finally had to admit he didn't honestly know. What he did know was that God spared him.

Farther and farther north David and Ramotobi trudged. They visited every village, inspecting it for water, food, and fever. David did not find one healthful place for white families. He faithfully mapped the region, collected samples, and kept his journal. Everywhere he went, he made friends and preached the gospel.

Coming behind him were

| GUESS |

1. white slave traders.
2. more rhinos.
3. elephants.

The slave traders were behind him. At first, they were trying to catch him to kill him. Failing to do that, they said, "We are Livingstone's sons." At once the natives opened their hearts and fed the strangers. In the morning, the slavers asked for a group of porters, twenty to thirty young people. Everyone volunteered, and the slavers picked out the strongest.

As soon as they were out of sight of the village, the slavers had the natives cut branches that were forked. The slavers drilled a hole in each section of the branch about five inches below the fork. At a given signal, they tied up the natives, and one by one placed the yoke over the back of their necks. By sliding an iron rod through the holes and fastening it, they yoked each native by the neck. Weighed down by the slave sticks, they were unable to run away. Then the slave traders led them to the sea, forced them into their ships, and sailed away to America.

David found out

GUESS	1. that day.
	2. that month.
	3. much, much later.

Because David and Ramotobi traveled so much farther than the Boers, David did not discover their treachery until much later.

By May 1853, David reached Linyanti, capital of Makololo. Still he had not found a suitable location for a mission station. "Perhaps I should go to the right or left, and then I might find a highway to the sea."

But Ramotobi wanted to go home. "I can find the way, Master," he said.

David parted with his faithful companion, letting him go with God's blessing and a compass.

11

Go West

Linyanti was a large village, and David had been there before. All seven thousand natives rushed to meet him. They

GUESS

1. shouted.
2. waved branches.
3. screeched to one another.

Showing rows of white teeth in thousands of smiles, the natives shouted and waved branches. They pulled David along to see their new king, the eighteen-year-old son of Seibituane, David's old friend.

"Sekeluta, our new king," they cried. "Sekeluta, Sekeluta."

David bowed politely. The king also bowed and held out his hands in greeting.

"Father always honored you, Dr. Livingstone. So do I. What is your reason for coming?"

"As always, to preach to your people of the God in heaven, who loves you, and His Son, Jesus." David paused. "I am also looking for a good place to build a mission and a way to the sea. If your people had a way to get the ivory to the coast, they could trade it for tools."

"Like plows?" Sekeluta asked.

"Like plows," David answered.

"Very well, we will help you. Name anything you require, and I will get it for you."

David asked for

GUESS

1. a sheepskin cloak.
2. a horse rug.
3. an opportunity to help the people become Christians.

When David said he wanted the natives to study the Bible, the king hung his head.

"But I do not wish to know the Bible."

"Why not? Your father was interested," David responded.

"I know, but he couldn't be Christian because he wouldn't give up any of his five wives. I do not want to be Christian, either. I want at least five wives like my father—maybe more. If I study the Bible, it may teach otherwise," Sekeluta stated.

David could see the king was not ready for the gospel. It was not his way to force anyone. He just held out his hands and smiled, saying nothing.

He accepted the canoe that Sekeluta offered him. He accepted the ten fine elephant tusks the king gave him, and then he presented them one by one to ten natives to sell for themselves.

Finally, he turned to the king, smiled, and said, "One day I hope you will see your mistake and turn to Christ, who will be waiting for you."

It was good that David was among friends, for

GUESS

1. he was lonely.
2. he became ill.
3. he needed help.

When he was better, the natives killed an ox and cut the meat into long strips, which they threw into the fire. They served it to David half cooked and burning hot. They could not understand why he chewed it so long. The Makololo's idea was to get as much food as possible into their stomachs, rather than to enjoy the flavor.

They also brought a container of milk. This they scooped up by hand and drank. When David gave them some iron spoons, they dipped the milk with the spoon, then poured the milk into their hands and drank. It was much too slow to please them, but they loved the spoons for beating drums.

"Why, oh, why, did I give them spoons?" David cried, holding his aching head.

David's strength returned, so that by September he was making preparations to go west to find a highway to the sea. Sekeluta appointed twenty-seven men to go with him as carriers. "I want you to promise to bring them all back safely."

David spoke,

GUESS	1. "I promise to bring them back."
	2. "They can find jobs on the coast and live there."
	3. "I want to go home to see my children."

David looked into the young king's eyes and said, "I promise to bring your men home again."

The porters carried a few beads for presents, some medicines, a few biscuits, sugar, tea and coffee, a tent, a sheepskin cloak and a horsehair rug, guns and ammunition for shooting game to eat, some clothing, a magic lantern,* a thermometer and compasses, a Bible, map paper, writing materials, boxes for samples, and instruments for making astronomical observations—so they wouldn't get lost.

The porters also carried canoes on their heads.

Soon they were paddling up the Zambezi River. The chanting could be heard for miles. When they came to the falls, local natives slung the canoes on poles and carried them overland. Beyond the falls, the porters discovered that the local people had filled the canoes with meat, meal, butter, and milk. They waved their thanks to the strangers, who waved and smiled, teeth glistening in the sun.

The porters

*Old fashioned slide projector.

GUESS

1. cut grass for David's bed at night.
2. pitched a tent.
3. built a large fire.

The porters not only did all that, they arranged his boxes under the tent so they too would be dry.

Day after day they followed the river. All around them, the tropical forest closed in. As David peered into the depths, he said,

GUESS

1. "The river is dwindling to a stream."
2. "Soon we will leave the river."
3. "Soon we will plunge into the jungle."

David feared the time when they must leave the river.

Local chiefs greeted the procession with hospitality. David returned their good will but was almost smothered by a large female chief.

GUESS

1. Her body was smeared with fat and red color.
2. She wore many ornaments.
3. She was just like Mary.

No one could be more different from Mary! The red color and many ornaments covered her body. She had never seen white skin and straight hair. She wanted to feel them.

David tried to ignore her and presented her with an ox. At once the lady chief pounced on it, saying, "It is mine. The ox is mine and so is the white man! I am Manenko, big chief!" She patted her stomach and ordered the ox cooked.

David showed his "magic lantern" and flashed a slide on the screen. That quieted everyone until he showed a picture of Abraham about to kill his son, Isaac. At that Manenko ran from the place, shouting, "Mother, Mother!"

After she was gone, David and her uncle Shinte visited. David tried to present the gospel. Shinte clapped his hands and nodded his head to everything, but David could see he understood nothing of the message of Christ.

Before David left on January 26, 1854, Shinte gave him

GUESS	1. a razor.
---	2. a string of beads.
	3. a special shell.

The special shell was the same as a key to the city. He also sent guides to take him across a swampy plain to the Kasci River. David drew the Kasci River on the map.

David decided

GUESS	1. to follow the river north.
---	2. to cross the river and continue on land.
	3. to go back.

David didn't know that the Kasci River joined the mighty Congo. He did know the coast of Africa was westward, so far west that they marched straight into the jungle lands of Chief Katende.

Chief Katende said, "You cannot pass over my land unless you pay. Pay me

GUESS	1. a man [to be a slave]."
---	2. a tusk of ivory."
	3. beads, copper rings, and a shell."

Katende demanded all that.

David entered a lengthy bargaining session. Back and forth the discussion went, until finally the chief settled for beads and one of David's shirts.

Only a few days later, David's group entered Chiboque country. There the natives thought they improved their looks by filing their teeth to a point. They demanded

GUESS	1. a shirt.
	2. more beads.
	3. a handkerchief.

Every time the chief made a demand his followers rushed into a circle around David, spears upheld. One made a charge from behind. David quickly turned and pointed the muzzle of his gun at the native's mouth. He glared at the young man, who slunk away. David turned around the entire circle, pointing his gun. Slowly, the natives vanished, and David's party continued on their way. The natives knew the power of the gun.

Over and over David grew desperately ill. When he was too weak to walk farther, he climbed onto an ox named Sinbad. He was so dizzy he didn't notice the branches that hung down over the gloomy path in the dark forest. When he was brushed off the ox's back by a branch, Sinbad seemed to be pleased to kick his master as he lay on the ground.

The porters

GUESS	1. rescued him.
	2. made camp.
	3. cooked his food.

The porters did all those things for David, and in a few days the travelers continued on their way.

As they drew closer to the coast, each chief demanded more pay. The porters had been obliged to part with nearly all their ornaments. Many were sick, and all were discouraged with the damp, dark forest and the never ceasing rain.

After conferring, the porters said to David,

GUESS	1. "Let us go home."
	2. "We have decided to take you home."
	3. "Will you go on alone?"

David answered,

GUESS

1. "I'm too sick to care anymore."
2. "I want to go home, too."
3. "I will go on alone."

After telling the porters he was going on alone, David went into his tent and fell into bed. Soon he heard shuffling feet. "We will never leave you. Do not be disheartened. Wherever you lead, we will follow." The tent was crowded with porters. "We are all your children. We will die for you." David was too sick to talk. He smiled and held out his hands.

On March 30, they came to a sudden descent from the high land. The hillside was so steep that David left Sinbad's back and, held up by two porters, staggered to the bottom.

David stumbled out of the gloom of the trees into the glorious light of the Quango Valley. He felt better just looking over

GUESS

1. hundreds of miles without jungle.
2. green grass meadows.
3. a river sparkling in the sun.

Though all those things were beautiful, the people who lived in the area were just as demanding as the other tribes. One chief asked for a red jacket and one of the porters for a slave.

David tried to reason with him. "We have no red jacket, and these porters are free men." The porters tried to give the last of their copper rings. David saw that these natives had guns.

He tried to hide in his tent to let the angry tempers cool, but the tent was in tatters. He finally rose and suggested they move on. At that moment a young half-caste Portuguese sergeant of the militia made his appearance. He encouraged the porters to go. Frightened that they would be shot in the back, they hurried. When the natives did fire their bullets fell short, and David's men reached the river safely.

"Thank You, God," David rejoiced.

The sergeant led them, sick, wet, and hungry, the rest of the journey. He stopped at a Portuguese militia station where they were invited to a breakfast of

91

GUESS

1. ground nuts.
2. roasted maize.
3. boiled manioc roots.

All that, with guavas and honey as dessert, was included in a meal David wrote home about.

When David walked into St. Paul de Luanda on the west coast of Africa, June 1854, he was a skeleton. His clothes were in tatters, and he was suffering his twenty-seventh attack of fever. He wrote Joseph Moore, "You cannot imagine the delight of lying on a comfortable bed after seven months of sleeping on the wet ground."

The British Consul in Luanda cared for David until he regained his strength, and the Portuguese traders cared for his porters.

"There is a ship bound for England leaving soon," the consul said. "Your porters have put all your samples and maps aboard. Will you be going, too?"

It had been two years since David said good-bye to Mary and the children.

David decided

GUESS

1. to go to England at once because he had been ill.
2. to stay on the coast.
3. to go back to Makololo with the porters.

David could not break his promise. He turned his back on the blue, blue ocean and the ship that might have taken him home.

"I have not found a suitable place for a mission or a highway to the sea. My work is not finished. I promised these twenty-seven men I would take them back. I cannot go to England. I would not be glorifying God."

For the trip back, he was given a new tent, plenty of guns, and generous presents for Sekeluta, including a splendid uniform.

The hardships of the trip to the coast repeated themselves on the way back. Sleeping on the wet ground gave David rheumatic fever. He wrote, "There was no help for it. Every part of the plain was flooded ankle deep." He put his watch under his armpit to keep it dry from the rain. They lived on manioc roots and meal. On

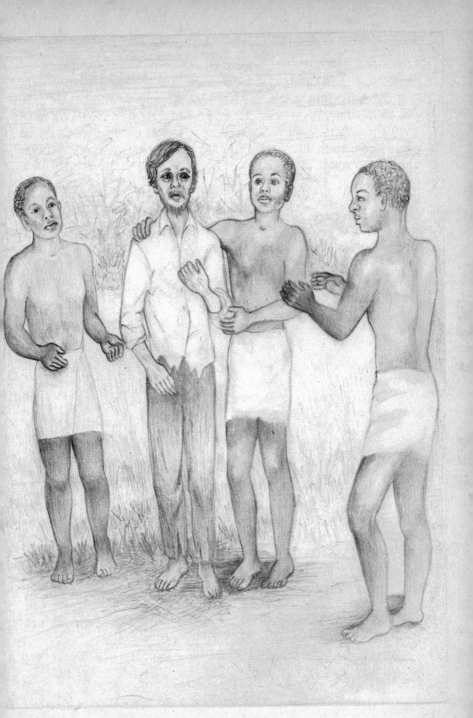

David reaches the African west coast.

the days it didn't rain, it was 96 degrees in the shade.

But they did make it home, all twenty-eight of them. On July 23, 1855, almost two years from the day they started, David gave the young chief Sekeluta his uniform. He was so entranced that he wore it to church, and David noted that it "attracted more attention than the sermon."

12

Go East

For two months David rested in Linyanti surrounded by good friends.

On November 3, 1855, he was ready to follow the Zambezi River eastward. "Who will go with me?" he asked his Makololo friends. "Step forward if you will go."

GUESS

1. 114 stepped forward.
2. 27 stepped forward.
3. 10 stepped forward.

As 114 stepped forward, David asked, "Why? Why so many? Remember the days of starvation, the unfriendly tribes, the rain and the sickness? Have you forgotten the steaming hot wet days?"

Sekelutu, the young chief, smiled. "They have been collecting elephant tusks and want to sell them on the coast."

"And they are willing to carry the equipment, maps, samples, and letters?" David asked.

"They are willing, Doctor. I, myself, will go a short way. I'd like to see strange places, too."

David thought he had a parade before; now he had a caravan. The natives had made canoes and gathered supplies. This time they knew

GUESS	1. they needed blankets of skin to keep out dampness.
	2. boots must be watertight.
	3. many beads were needed.

Not long after they put their canoes into the water, they came upon the beautiful Mosi-oa-tunya, which David named Victoria Falls for the English queen. David wrote in his journal, "Columns of vapour rise above the tumbling waters and are imbued by the sun with the colours of the rainbow. The banks are covered with trees of different colour, being showered with a fine spray. 'Tis dramatically beautiful."

They saw

GUESS	1. buffaloes and elands.
	2. hartebeests and gnus.
	3. elephants.

All of these animals were tame, since no one disturbed them.

Sekeluta could hardly say good-bye, he was so entranced by the strange sights. "God bless you!" he repeated David's words to him. Livingstone smiled. "Someday you, too, will believe."

After they crossed the Kalomo River, they neared the first unfriendly village. One of the villagers dashed forward howling at the top of his voice in a hideous manner. His eyeballs protruded; his lips were covered with foam. He slung a battle-ax over the white man's head.

David felt

GUESS	1. fearful.
	2. brave.
	3. excited.

David admitted in his journal, "I felt a little alarmed, but would not show fear before my own people or strangers. I did keep a sharp lookout on the little battle-ax. I felt it would be a sorry way to

96

leave the world, to get my head chopped off by a mad savage."

When the chief saw that David was not afraid,

GUESS	1. he called off the villager.
	2. he sneered at them.
	3. he kissed them all.

Because none of the Makololo had spears, the chief thought them foolish.

"You have wandered to be destroyed—weaklings!" the chief taunted.

At a signal from David, the Makololo fired their guns in the air.

The chief suddenly showed respect and let the caravan pass.

David wrote, "If we really had a battle, the Makololos' guns would be more trouble than good for they do not know how to shoot straight."

The farther east they went the more tribes they met. Having never seen a white man, the natives came to stare at the procession.

But farther east, more warlike tribes had been fighting the Portuguese settlers at Tete for two years and distrusted all white men.

Chief Mpende sent two warriors to ask, "Who are you?"

David answered, "I am a *Lekoa,* an Englishman."

"We do not know that tribe. We thought you were Portuguese."

David showed them his hair and skin.

"No, we never saw skin so white," one warrior said.

"You must be one of the tribe that loves black men," the other spoke up.

David joyfully agreed, and they were allowed to pass without trouble. By cutting across a loop in the Zambezi River, the group found two healthy ridges at the mouth of the Loangwa River. "Now at last, I've found a good place for a mission. The directors of the London Missionary Society will surely want to build here." David rejoiced.

They arrived on the east coast May 20, 1856. When they entered Quelimane, David was hailed as the first European to have crossed Africa coast to coast.

"It was only with God's care and protection I was able to make the crossing," David declared.

David heard of a ship arriving soon to unload and return to England. He decided

1. to settle the porters in Tete.
2. to send the porters back without him.
3. to forget about the 114 porters.

David went back to Tete with the 114 porters and helped them get settled. He promised to take every one back to Makololo when he returned from England. The porters felt rich with the money they had from the sale of their elephant tusks.

When the ship arrived, David received a letter from the London Missionary Society. "Due to financial circumstances we cannot venture to undertake untried or remote and difficult fields of labor." David was crushed.

He thought,

1. *God helped me find a good place for a station.*
2. *God helped me find a highway to the coast.*
3. *God will help me build a mission.*

David glorified God.

13

Coming Home

When David's ship docked in England in December 1856, the first to greet him was

GUESS

1. Mary.
2. his four children.
3. Joseph Moore.

Mary greeted him first. He stood each child up on the rail beside the gangplank. "I can't believe this tall lad is Robert. How could Nannie have grown so much?" Even baby Agnes was now five years old. He hugged all four children. "Oh, thank You, God, for taking care of my family. I did the right thing to send you home, Mary. I see it now, but oh, how I missed you."

They all climbed into a carriage, and the horses took them home. "Tell us about your adventure," Robert shyly requested. David

GUESS

1. talked till midnight.
2. told of the seven times his life was threatened.
3. just told of the discoveries.

David mostly told of his discoveries. But he also learned that his father had died a short time ago. Accordingly, they all packed up and left for Scotland a few days later.

The sight of his mother, his father's empty chair, Blantrye, Shuttle Row, and his sisters and brothers overwhelmed him.

While the sisters and brothers were playing with his children, David drew Mary to the platform at the top of the spiral staircase. "Remember when I asked you to come see my Scottish hills, the River Clyde, and even the old Blantrye Works?"

Mary answered, "So much has happened since then."

They held each other close as the chilly breeze whipped by.

As they were leaving for London, Charlie rushed up to David. "One thing I forgot to tell you—people go to Bothwell Castle

1. to see your name carved on the wall."
2. to pick flowers."
3. to study the stars."

"Why," David gasped, "would anyone want to see my name?"

"You don't know! You be famous now!" Charlie marveled.

As soon as they returned to London, David was forced to admit his fame. He was asked to speak by

1. travelers and geographers.
2. zoologists and astronomers.
3. physicians and merchants.

All those people wanted to hear of his adventures. David

1. refused to speak.
2. made as many speeches as requested.
3. hid away from people.

David accepted every opportunity to speak. "I'll tell them of God's mercy, of the discoveries, the riches of Africa, the fine rivers, and the beautiful animals. But I'll never make a speech without telling them of the slave traders and how they put slave sticks over the shoulders of my people. This slave trade must be stopped."

People in England became alarmed about slavery. Merchants from America listened to him, and they

GUESS	1. went back to North America.
	2. told of the evils of slavery.
	3. kept quiet.

Everyone was talking. No one was quiet.

The things that David said in London were repeated in Boston, Philadelphia, and New York. The word spread. "Something must be done about slavery!" became the cry.

When honors were heaped upon David, he received them humbly. "I am happy for this honor, but I would be more happy to hear that slavery is no more. Down with slavery! Down with slavery!" he cried.

He received a summons to tell his story before the king and queen of England. He was

GUESS	1. too bashful to accept.
	2. afraid to speak before royalty.
	3. glad for the opportunity.

David told them of crossing Africa. "I did it to glorify God, to find locations for mission stations, to find highways for missionaries and merchants. There was only one close behind me, the slave trader.

"When I was on the east coast of Africa, I saw the slaves being loaded into ships. I saw body after body lying on the ground where the loading was taking place. As a doctor, I examined them for the cause of death. There was only one cause—a broken heart. My people would rather die than be slaves."

The newspapers were full of news of David Livingstone, his feats, his discoveries, his warnings of slavery. The newspapers found their way to the United States. People in the North said, "The time has come. We must stop slavery."

Everyone begged David to write a book. Most of 1857 he spent at home with Mary and the children. From his journals, he could have written ten books, but he wrote only one. It was mostly about

GUESS

1. plants and animals.
2. rocks and geography.
3. missionary work and travel.

David found room for all of those in his book called *Missionary Travels.* When it came out, everyone wanted a copy.

Even before David had finished his book, he was itching to get back to his missionary work. "I would rather cross Africa than write another book," he said.

At Cambridge University, he made a speech about opening up a path to commerce and Christianity. "If you knew the joy of duty and the gratitude to God a missionary feels to be chosen, you, too, would want to go. . . . I go back to Africa to serve. You, too, can serve God. I leave it with you to decide."

The people who heard this speech said, "Let us start a missionary society—the Universities Mission for Christian Work. David Livingstone must never

GUESS

1. be short of supplies.
2. lack for money.
3. be hungry again.

David felt it best not to accept money from the London Missionary Society, and he accepted a position from the English government as consul. Also, he agreed to command an expedition for exploring the eastern and central portions of Africa.

David's visit to London

GUESS

1. frightened people.
2. changed ideas about African missions.
3. changed ideas about blacks and slavery.

102

The only frightened people were the slave traders.

David sailed back to Africa on March 10, 1858. Because of him,

1. merchants were interested in Africa.
2. scientists were interested in Africa.
3. Christians were interested in Africa.

All wanted to help.

14

Slavers

David's first task upon his return was to take the porters he had left in Tete back up the Zambezi River. To his surprise, some

GUESS	1. refused to go back.
	2. started back, then deserted.
	3. went back to Makololo.

David was somewhat ashamed to return to Makololo with so few porters. When he found Sekeluta, David was shocked, for

GUESS	1. the young king looked old.
	2. the king didn't know him.
	3. the king had leprosy.

Because of his leprosy, Sekeluta secluded himself in a covered wagon behind a high wall of reeds. Now he was willing to listen to David tell him of Christ, who died to save his soul.

"Your body is dying," David said, "but your soul will soon be

free to go to Jesus in heaven if you will only believe."
Sekeluta

1. believed.
2. refused to listen.
3. said, "It is too late."

Sekeluta believed. When David held a meeting for all the natives in Linyanti that day, many others also accepted the gospel.

David hurried back down the Zambezi to the Shire Valley where he had found the healthful lands. *I must tell of this in a book,* he thought.

On September 16, 1859, seven missionaries arrived, and David helped them start a mission in Zanzibar. With the missionaries came

GUESS
1. Joseph Moore.
2. Charles Livingstone.
3. James Young.

David was surprised and delighted to see his little brother, Charles. Along with Doctor Kirk, the three sailed up the Loangwa River to Lake Nyasa. They paid the local people to carry their boat across.

The pay to the natives was

GUESS
1. ten beads.
2. many yards of cloth.
3. tin cans.

The natives loved cloth and immediately wrapped it around themselves. David thought it better than beads. On September 2, 1861, the explorers felt cool air as they rounded a mountain and came upon a cape, which they named Cape Maclear.

All around the lake, native villages flourished. As their little boat sailed past, dark crowds stood on the sand gazing at them.

When they landed, hundreds of natives came to stare at

GUESS

1. the chirambo (wild animals with wings).
2. the dead people walking (whites).
3. the jabos.

The natives called them chirambo (wild animals with wings) for they had never seen white men in sailboats before. They smiled when David tried to speak. *Someday I must learn their language,* David thought.

When the three explorers returned seven months later with a larger boat, the villages on the banks stood silent. Skeletons lay beside the paths. Outside some huts, a few boys and girls crouched, watching listlessly. Dead bodies floated past the steamer as the crocodiles fought over them.

"What happened?" Charles cried.

David answered,

GUESS

1. "A cyclone came."
2. "The slavers have taken them all."
3. "Those who fought were killed."

Charles choked, "You mean the slave traders either killed or took all these kind, gentle people?"

When they found that the slavers had gained the confidence of the people by pretending to be David's children, Charles and Dr. Kirk asked permission to go home. They had seen enough.

Later, David and a large group were on their way from Chibisa when they overtook a long line of natives led by black drivers. When the black drivers saw them, they ran into the jungle. David and his friends saw that each native had his neck in the fork of a six-or-seven-foot stick. As an iron rod riveted at both ends held the men's throats, it was necessary to saw the wooden forks to free them.

Livingstone's men cut the ropes off the women and children. One of the men could speak a tongue known to David and told of two women who had been shot the night before for trying to free

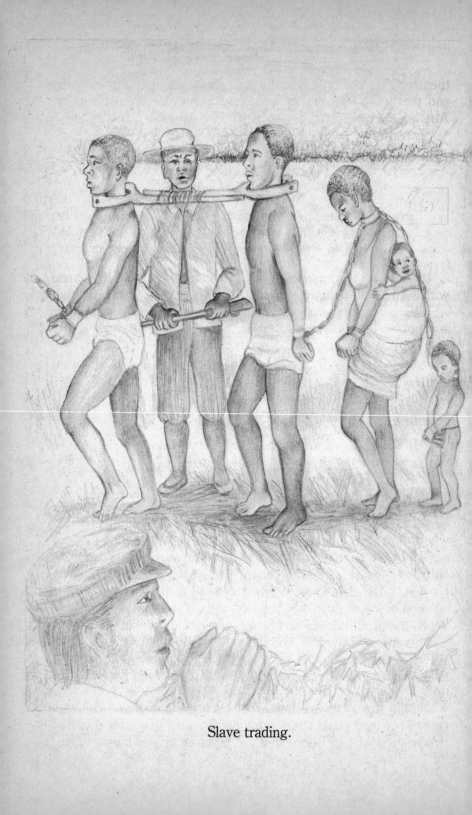

Slave trading.

themselves. Another woman found it impossible to carry her baby and the heavy load on her head, so the slavers killed the baby. Another old man could not keep up. He was hit with an ax.

David felt

 GUESS

1. angry.
2. miserable.
3. happy.

The anger and misery in David's soul were shared by everyone with him. "Wait until we tell about this in London," they promised.

When the captives were told they could go home now, they stayed close to David's people. They wouldn't go because

GUESS

1. they were afraid.
2. they would be captured again.
3. they trusted Livingstone.

The native, who could speak one of David's languages, explained, "If they leave you, they will just be captured again and treated worse than before."

David decided to take them to the new mission in Zanzibar where they would be safe and happy.

The slavers, however, said to the natives, "See, Livingstone only sets you free so that he can make you slaves for his religion. He is worse than we are. We take you to kind masters."

David feared no one would believe him anymore. He wrote in his journal:

"Small children were usually tied with ropes and walked along with the other slaves with great endurance. When they passed a village, they would hear the sound of dancing or the tinkle of the drums. Then the reminder of happy days was too much, and they would cry with a broken heart. Soon, they would die."

David had dreams at night of

| GUESS |

1. fun.
2. the evils of slavery.
3. crying children.

15

Stanley

With plenty of supplies and porters, David explored the Rovuma River in March 1866.
He found

<table>
<tr><td>GUESS</td><td>1. the guide was a liar.
2. the jungle was wet.
3. dead bodies tied to trees.</td></tr>
</table>

David found all those along the way, along with heaps of human bones and wooden collars, indicating that the Arab slave traders had been there. "I must write another book," David said.

David paid off some of his unreliable porters. Others feared the slave traders and abandoned their supplies on the ground, running away and telling people everywhere, "Livingstone is dead." By December, he had only a few men and fewer supplies. Two porters remained as his true friends. Chuma and Susi never left David, though he was weak and ill. Livingstone knew fresh supplies were being sent to Ujiji, so he continued in that direction. He contracted pneumonia, could hardly speak, and his feet were swollen. He kept on, though he seemed to see figures and faces in the bark of trees.

He staggered into Ujiji on March 14, 1869, only to find his

stores had been plundered and his medicines poured over the ground. For two more years he wandered, sick and without medicine.

Once, David was ambushed. A large spear grazed his back, then plunged into the earth. Another followed almost as close. Then guns were fired into the dense forest. Later he wrote, "Guns fired without effect for the forest was dark. We heard men jeering. I saw a gigantic tree, whose roots were eaten by fire. I heard a crack. As the tree fell toward me, I ran back. It shattered a yard behind me, as it hit the ground. Three times in one day, I was delivered from impending death."

On October 23, 1871, he returned to Ujiji to recover strength, using the supplies that he knew had been sent to him. When he arrived "reduced to a skeleton," he found that an Arab slave trader

GUESS	1. had sold his supplies.
	2. was waiting with his medicine.
	3. said, "I thought you were dead."

The Arab had sold his supplies and spent the money. "I will have to wait in beggary for help," David said. He didn't even have money to pay for food or wages for Chuma and Susi, who would not leave him.

Chuma managed to work for food for the three of them. Living in a tent, David was always busy writing in his journal, preparing samples, writing letters, and preaching.

In Ujiji, David preached to the Arabs. He stood in the marketplace with a semicircle of Arabs in front of him. David was pale, weary; his hair and beard had turned white. He wore a blue cap, a red-sleeved coat, and gray trousers.

When he looked up, he saw a white man with polished boots and flannel suit approaching.

"Doctor Livingstone, I presume!" he said.

"Yes," David said, smiling and lifting his cap. His preaching ended abruptly. He had not talked with a white man for six years.

Immediately, the two men walked back to the tent together. "I suppose the University's Mission sent you," David said.

"Oh, no, I was sent from the *New York Herald* in the United

States to find you. My name is Henry Stanley. Just call me Stanley."

Stanley came from New York, because

GUESS

1. he loved Livingstone.
2. he wanted a news story.
3. he was paid to find Livingstone.

"No amount of money would tempt me to travel those jungles," Stanley said later. "I was after a news story, but I found a friend."

When David told Stanley of the evils of slavery, Stanley said, "Oh, I was in the Civil War to help free the slaves in the South." David listened as Stanley told of the struggle. When he finished, he said, "I guess you know you helped to start the war."

"I? Impossible, I was here—never in America."

"No, but your words went to America. People heard of the evils of slavery and did something about it," Stanley stated.

David leaned forward. "They think it is over? They do not know that the Arabs are still capturing slaves every day!"

"No, tell me about it." Stanley took out his notebook. David looked back in his journals to get dates, places, facts. The two men worked into the wee hours.

"If these words lead to the end of the east coast slave trade, that will be more important than all my discoveries," David said.

Stanley wrote, "Livingstone is

GUESS

1. friendly and open."
2. noble and upright."
3. pious and manly."

All these words he said of David, and added, "To see and talk with Livingstone is to share in God's glory." To Stanley, David said, "You have brought me a new life."

Stanley brought

1. medicine.
2. news.
3. donkeys.

David appreciated the news Stanley brought; but most of all, he appreciated the fact that people in America cared and prayed for him. Stanley divided his clothes into two piles and gave David one. He divided all his goods, food, and medicines.

Together they made an exploratory trip to the northern shores of Lake Tanganyika, where they established that the Rusizi River flowed into the lake. David updated his maps for Stanley to take back, along with numerous samples.

In March 1872 Stanley said, "Come back to America with me!"

David answered, "I'll go as far as Tabora, but my work is not finished. I must go into the heart of Africa. No one knows what is there."

16
Rest

Five days after saying good-bye to Stanley, David celebrated his

GUESS	1. fifty-ninth birthday.
	2. twenty-fourth birthday.
	3. fortieth birthday.

David was fifty-nine years old, and his hair and beard were white. He dressed up in Stanley's fine clothes; Susi cooked a good meal; David wrote in his journal, "March 19th—Birthday. My Jesus, my King, my Life, my All; I again dedicate my whole self to Thee."

In May he wrote a letter to the *New York Herald* begging Americans to stop the east coast slave trade. Americans had just fought to free their slaves and were furious that slavery was still going on.

Eventually, other countries also stopped slavery.

Day after day, David traveled to Lake Tanganyika, crossed the Kalongosi River, and climbed the mountains beyond. He descended north of Lake Bangweulu and explored the swampy shores where there were

GUESS
1. mosquitoes.
2. stinging ants.
3. poisonous spiders.

All of them attacked him. Once the fire ants followed him at night driving him from hut to hut until he fled into Lake Mweru to escape their ferocious bites.

Livingstone's sufferings were great. He

GUESS
1. was bleeding.
2. had dysentery.
3. had fever.

David suffered from all of the above. He wrote in his journal: "I am pale and weak, but, oh how I long to be permitted to finish my work."

By April 22, 1873, he was being carried on a litter.* On the night of April 30, he asked Susi how long before they would reach Luapula. He took his medicine, and said, "All right, you can go now."

A boy sleeping outside the tent peeked in during the night. He saw David kneeling by his bed, as though in prayer. In the morning, Susi found him in the same position. He was dead. David had fulfilled his promise to Dr. Prentice, "Though everyone else be dead and I myself sick, I would go on, and if I failed, I would at least die in the field."

Susi and Chumak now became the leaders of the company. First they allowed David's body to dry in the sun.

Chumak said, "We will take the body to the coast as Stanley instructed."

Susi agreed, "Yes, but we will not take the heart to England. His heart belongs to Africa, to us, his black people."

They buried his heart at the foot of a large tree, pounded two posts beside the tree and erected a crosspiece to join them. Chitambo said he would keep the grass cleared away.

*Stretcher.

116

They embalmed and wrapped the body in cloth, bent the legs inward at the knees, and covered the whole with a cylinder of bark. After sewing the bark in a piece of sailcloth, they lashed it to a carrying pole.

The natives

GUESS	1. put his papers in watertight boxes.
	2. loaded his scientific instruments.
	3. took animals with them.

The watertight boxes contained papers, maps, journals, and scientific instruments.

Five months later they arrived in Tabora. A party had been sent from England to relieve Livingstone. Verney Lovett Cameron tenderly accepted the body and boxes and returned everything to Zanzibar and finally to England.

Back in England some doubted this was the body of Livingstone, so an examination was made by medical authorities. "No one in the world has such a false joint as this in the arm crushed by the lion. There can be no doubt. These are the remains of one of the greatest men of the human race—David Livingstone."

At his funeral, he was praised for adding about a million square miles to the known portion of the globe, discovering several lakes, the Zambezi River, and Victoria Falls. He wrote two books. He was the first European to cross Africa west to east. He increased the knowledge of plants, animals, and geography without neglecting the extermination of the slave trade and the evangelization of Africa.

On April 18, 1874, his body was placed in Westminster Abbey, as crowds of people watched, including Robert Moffat. Near his grave, a tablet was erected. On it are the words he wrote one year before his death, "May Heaven's rich blessing come down on everyone, American, English or Turk, who will help to heal the open sore of the world."

By "open sore of the world," David meant

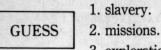 1. slavery.
2. missions.
3. exploration.

When David wrote that, he was pleading with men to end slavery all over the world.

David Livingstone had indeed lived his entire life to glorify God.

Moody Press, a ministry of the Moody Bible Institute, is designed for education, evangelization, and edification. If we may assist you in knowing more about Christ and the Christian life, please write us without obligation: Moody Press, c/o MLM, Chicago, Illinois 60610.